insight text guide

Ruth Thomas

The Rugmaker of Mazar-e-Sharif

Najaf Mazari & Robert Hillman

First published in 2009. Reprinted in 2010, 2011, 2012, 2021 (with revisions).

Insight Publications Pty Ltd
3/350 Charman Road
Cheltenham VIC 3192
Australia
Tel: +61 3 8571 4950
Fax: +61 3 8571 0257
Email: books@insightpublications.com.au

www.insightpublications.com.au

A catalogue record for this book is available from the National Library of Australia

Najaf Mazari & Robert Hillman's The Rugmaker of Mazar-e-sharif / Ruth Thomas

ISBNs:
9781921411038 (print)
9781925175240 (digital)
9781925175578 (bundle: print + digital)

Cover design by Gisela Beer

Printed in Australia by Ligare

contents

CHARACTER MAP

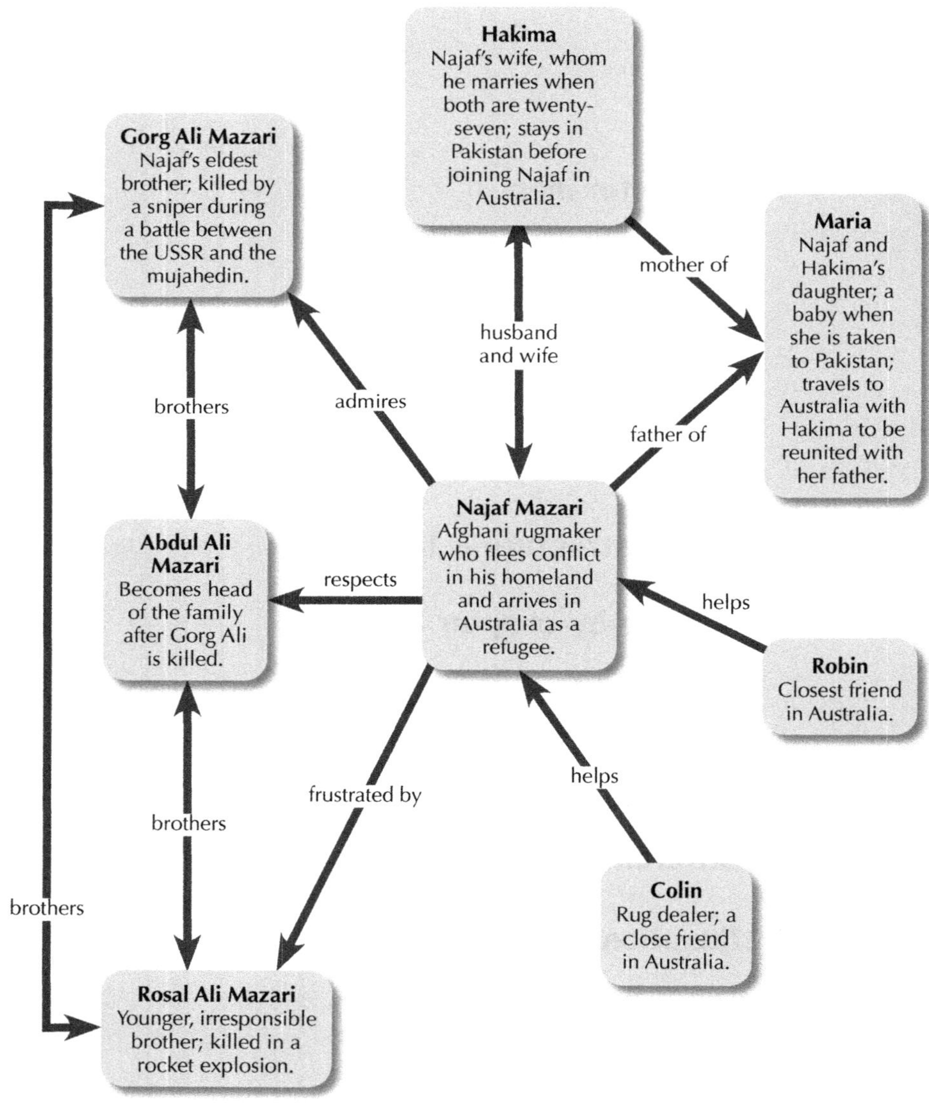

OVERVIEW

About the authors

Najaf Mazari was born in 1971 in the small village of Shar Shar in northern Afghanistan. At twelve years of age, after his family had moved to the city of Mazar-e-Sharif, Najaf became an apprentice rugmaker – an occupation that suited his propensity for both creativity and hard work. Seeing through his apprenticeship and aspiring to make beautiful rugs gave the young Najaf some respite from the horror of the incessant conflict around him.

In 2001, Najaf fled Afghanistan. The Taliban had occupied the north of the country and were carrying out genocide against men in Mazar-e-Sharif. Najaf was captured, tortured and narrowly escaped death, before his family paid a people smuggler to convey him out of the country. Najaf reluctantly left his family and his beloved homeland, and embarked on a dangerous journey to Australia. He was detained in the Woomera Detention Centre while his application for refugee status was processed. He then settled in Melbourne, where he opened a rug shop. In 2006, Najaf's wife and daughter were given permission by the Australian government to join him in Australia. He was granted Australian citizenship in 2007.

The Rugmaker of Mazar-e-Sharif is Najaf's memoir of living with conflict and of enduring its far-reaching consequences. Melbourne-based fiction writer and biographer Robert Hillman helps Najaf tell his story. Hillman's collaboration with Najaf on *The Rugmaker of Mazar-e-Sharif* continues his literary preoccupation with the hardships and triumphs of ordinary people caught up in war and political unrest. Hillman's 2007 biography, *My Life as a Traitor*, tells the story of Zarah Ghahramani, a young Iranian woman who was imprisoned, tortured and persecuted after participating in student protests at Tehran University. Hillman, who met Zarah while he was working as a journalist in Iran, supported her through her settlement as a refugee in Australia. His articles about refugees have been published in a number of newspapers and magazines, including *The New York Times* and *The Australian*. *My Life as a Traitor* has been published in the United States and the United Kingdom and was nominated for the 2008 Prime Minister's Literary Awards. Like *The Rugmaker of Mazar-e-Sharif, My Life as a Traitor* contains thoughtful meditations on Zarah's culture, which ensures that the book provides something more than a grim and shocking portrayal of war and suffering.

Hillman's autobiography, *The Boy in the Green Suit* (2003), a memoir about his own journey through the Middle East as a teenager, won the 2005 National Biography Award. The text was praised for its artfulness, evocation of restlessness, humour and optimism. His fiction has also been widely praised. It includes *A Life of Days* (1988), *The Hour of Disguise* (1990), *Writing Sparrow Hill* (1996) and *The Deepest Part of the Lake* (2001). An experienced teacher and university lecturer, Hillman also writes educational texts for secondary-school audiences.

Synopsis

Najaf's life begins in the small village of Shar Shar in northern Afghanistan, a place of hilly pastures, sunshine, snow, and bright green grass in spring. Najaf works as a shepherd boy, responsible for protecting the family's flock from wolves. Going to school comes second to his shepherding duties.

When Najaf is eight, his father dies and the family (now headed by Najaf's much-loved eldest brother, Gorg Ali) moves north to the city of Mazar-e-Sharif. Gorg Ali arranges an apprenticeship for Najaf when he turns twelve and is no longer, within Afghani culture, a boy; he is a young man ready to learn a trade. Najaf is first apprenticed to a blacksmith, but finds the work tedious and deeply unsatisfying. He secretly abandons his job to begin an apprenticeship under a master rugmaker. He quickly comes to love rugmaking and his passion for it offers a sanctuary from the war that rages around him.

His work, however, does not shield him from the reality of conflict. War inflicts terrible personal costs on young Najaf. Gorg Ali is gunned down in a battle between Soviet Union and mujahedin fighters in Shar Shar. Najaf's younger brother, Rosal Ali, is killed when a mortar shell explodes over the family home in the middle of the night. Najaf is injured in the attack and his apprenticeship jeopardised because the wound to his leg takes many months to heal. Najaf is just thirteen when he endures these terrible experiences.

Although he is a civilian and remains staunchly opposed to violence throughout his life, conflict continues to impact upon Najaf during adulthood. In 1998, the Taliban invade Mazar-e-Sharif. The Taliban massacre men and boys of Najaf's Hazara clan and then capture and torture any survivors they find. Now married with a baby daughter, Najaf is kidnapped and whipped with cables. However, to his and his family's disbelief, he is released.

Knowing he will not be so lucky a second time, Najaf escapes Afghanistan, putting his life in the hands of a people smuggler. The dangerous journey takes him through Afghanistan to Pakistan, then on to Indonesia and towards Australia on a condemnable boat. The boat eventually becomes stranded on Ashmore Reef, north of Australia. Najaf, along with other asylum seekers on board, is rescued by the Australian navy and conveyed to Woomera Detention Centre.

Here, Najaf endures the ordeal of waiting, his fate resting with immigration officials who will decide whether he has valid reason to stay in Australia. After months of detainment, Najaf is granted refugee status. He begins a life in Melbourne and, through hard work and hope, establishes a rug-selling business. More good news comes when Najaf is granted Permanent Residency Status, which not only means he can stay in Australia for good, but also that his wife, Hakima, and daughter, Maria, can move to Australia and join him in Melbourne.

Overwhelmed by happiness and appreciation for the seemingly impossible things that have happened, Najaf thanks God for his good fortune and promises to remember and honour those Afghanis who were not able to survive the country's violent conflicts.

Character summaries

Najaf Mazari

The central character and narrator, Najaf is in his mid-thirties when he tells his story. Over the course of the book he recounts his experiences as a young boy, teenager and young man. He is less than eight years old when working as a shepherd boy in Shar Shar and about twelve when he begins his rugmaking apprenticeship.

Gorg Ali

Najaf's much-admired eldest brother. In keeping with Afghani tradition, Gorg Ali takes over as head of the family when Najaf's father dies. Gorg Ali is a gentle man who believes that fighting is senseless and futile. He works as a tinsmith and a beekeeper. He is killed by a stray bullet when he goes to tend the family beehives near Shar Shar.

Abdul Ali

Najaf's second-eldest brother. When Gorg Ali dies, Abdul Ali becomes the head of the family and bears the financial burden that results from the mortar attack on the family's home. He is more hot-headed than Gorg Ali and subjects Najaf to several blows about the head when he discovers Najaf has secretly quit his job as a blacksmith. Abdul Ali is a butcher.

Rosal Ali

Najaf's younger brother. Rosal Ali is hopelessly irresponsible, mischievous and cheeky. He often provokes Najaf's anger. Najaf, as the older brother, lectures Rosal Ali. Rosal Ali is killed when the Mazaris' home is destroyed in the mortar attack.

Najaf's mother

An important member of the Mazari family. Najaf's mother has the final say on her son's marriage plans and rules the inside of the house in partnership with the head of the family. In turn, Najaf is respectful to his mother and often acts protectively towards her. Najaf sees his mother (and the rest of his family) on a number of occasions after leaving Afghanistan, when he undertakes rug-buying trips to Pakistan.

Hakima

Najaf's wife. She is the same age as Najaf; they marry at the age of twenty-seven. Hakima stays in Pakistan between 2001, when Najaf flees Afghanistan, and 2006, when she is granted permission by the Australian government to join Najaf in Australia.

Maria

Najaf and Hakima's daughter. Maria is just a baby when Najaf sends her and Hakima to safety in Pakistan. She is reunited with her father five years later.

Robin

An Australian woman who becomes Najaf's closest friend in Australia. She helps Najaf learn English and holds a party to celebrate his achievements in his new home.

Colin

A Melbourne rug dealer who helps Najaf with his business. He drives Najaf to the airport to be reunited with Hakima and Maria.

BACKGROUND & CONTEXT

Conflict in Afghanistan

Najaf's homeland has a long history of violent and bitter armed conflict that spans centuries. This is partly due to the region's geography. As Najaf says, 'just look at the location of Afghanistan on a map of Asia and the Middle East, with neighbours and near-neighbours like Russia, Pakistan and Iran' (p.34). The area has enormous geographical and strategic significance. Foreign powers, from the ancient Macedonians through to the colonial British and communist Soviet Union, have striven to secure territory or allies there, with little regard for the desires of the local people. Anger towards foreign invaders is evident in Najaf's observation that Afghanistan and Afghanis were 'supposed to fit into the political strategies of the powerful' (p.35). Afghanis tried to fight off invaders, and also fought each other as various tribal and ethnic groups each attempted to stake out their own parcels of territory.

In the period from 1973 to 2000, five separate conflicts took place in Afghanistan, including civil wars (armed conflict between opposing parties within one country) and international wars (armed conflict between two or more countries). This particularly turbulent period commenced when Mohammad Daoud Khan assumed power in a military coup. Daoud failed to deliver much-needed economic and social reform and was ultimately overthrown in a second coup in 1978. This uprising was led by the Marxist Nur Mohammad Taraki, who implemented a liberal and socialist agenda, replacing religious and traditional laws with secular, Marxist ones. Taraki was soon ousted by Hafizullah Amin, who was in turn replaced in yet another coup by Babrak Karmal. Najaf recalls that, by the time he was thirteen, Afghanistan had been ruled by four presidents, all of whom represented the Communist Party (pp.149–50).

Karmal was supported by the Soviet Union, or controlled by it, as Najaf suggests (p.11), and continued to implement Marxist reforms.

While many people in the cities either approved of these changes or were ambivalent about them, many traditional and conservative Afghanis in villages and rural areas were bitterly opposed. Opposition groups, known as mujahedin ('holy Muslim warrior'), began to form. The mujahedin belonged to different factions but shared, to varying degrees, a conservative Islamic ideology. They also shared a serious commitment to fighting. Najaf remembers a mujahedin leader who was so badly wounded during a battle that 'one of his eyes was blown from its socket and dangled down his cheek' (p.36). But, rather than surrender, this man simply 'cut the eye from his face with his knife and resumed the fight' (p.36).

The Afghan army was unable to deal with the increasing number of violent incidents perpetrated by the mujahedin throughout the country, so the Soviet Union sent in troops to crush the uprisings. The clashes between the mujahedin and the Soviet forces were violent and unpredictable, and regularly impacted upon civilians (people who take no active part in fighting). It is during battles between these two forces that Gorg Ali is killed and the high-explosive rocket destroys the Mazaris' home, killing Rosal Ali and injuring Najaf. The Soviet troops stayed in Afghanistan until 1989. When they withdrew, Afghanistan was plunged into a civil war where mujahedin forces, which had coexisted uneasily during the Soviet occupation, fought against each other for power.

In 1994, a new force emerged. Comprising young religious scholars who were also brilliant guerrilla fighters, this force took the name 'Taliban' ('pious scholars'). Religious fervour, tactical brilliance and a dedication to fighting meant the Taliban controlled almost all of Afghanistan by 1998. Their leader, Mohammad Omar, declared Afghanistan an Islamic Republic and instituted a raft of oppressive reforms, particularly severe in relation to women's rights. Under Taliban rule, women were effectively restricted to the home, denied education and could be executed for failing to observe the strict dress code. In late 2001, the Taliban were driven out of power by a United States–led invasion, instigated in response to the September 11 terrorist attacks in America. Democratic elections were held in 2004 and Hamid Karzai was elected president under a new constitution.

The Taliban, however, still operates in Afghanistan as an insurgency, and currently controls sections of the country. The Afghan government has received military support from a number of countries, including Australia, to help combat the Taliban. Najaf, with his knowledge of how conflict plays out in Afghanistan, is not confident that the foreign armies will enjoy ultimate success in his homeland. Taliban fighters, he observes, 'have only their mission, which is victory' (p.251). Ten years, a long time to fight for Australian or American soldiers, is nothing to Taliban fighters to whom 'even a hundred years is not a long time' to fight (p.251).

Refugees and asylum seekers

Millions of people have been displaced by the decades of conflict in Afghanistan. People who flee war zones or other areas of conflict because they fear persecution or death are known as refugees. But the word is much more than a label. It is actually a legal term that conveys significant and important rights to a victim of armed conflict.

The term 'refugee' is defined in a key international treaty: the United Nations Convention Relating to the Status of Refugees. This Convention defines a refugee as any person who:

> owing to a well-founded fear of being persecuted for reasons of race, religion, nationality, membership of a particular social group, or political opinion, is outside the country of his or her nationality, and is unable to or, owing to such fear, is unwilling to avail himself or herself of the protection of that country.

In short, it means a person is a refugee if they are forced to flee their home because their identity puts them in danger. The Convention goes on to state the rights of refugees and to stipulate the obligations of other countries when refugees seek safety within their borders.

There are 193 member states of the United Nations. A majority of those countries, including Australia, has signed the Convention, thereby agreeing to observe their obligations set out within it. These obligations require signatory nations to accept refugees who enter that country's borders or territorial waters. Once within that country's borders, people cannot be deported if they prove themselves to be genuine refugees. Under the Convention, genuine refugees must be allowed to stay in the country in which they have arrived.

In practice, many countries party to the Convention have implemented independent procedures and conditions for accepting refugees. This has resulted in the evolution of the term 'asylum seeker' to distinguish between someone whose claim to refugee status has been legitimately established, and someone whose claim is yet to be proved. An asylum seeker, simply, is a person who is seeking safety in a country other than their own and who claims to be a refugee. Najaf is an asylum seeker when he is rescued from Ashmore Reef. He is still an asylum seeker during his detention in Woomera. He is a refugee, according to Australian law, when he is granted a visa and allowed to settle in Melbourne. This visa is only granted after Najaf proves his claims through many interviews and after numerous identity and evidence checks have been conducted in Afghanistan.

Initially, Najaf is granted a Temporary Protection Visa. That document allows him to stay in Australia until the government deems it safe for him to return to Afghanistan. Najaf is later given Permanent Residency Status, permitting him to stay in his new country permanently, to become a citizen and to bring Hakima and Maria to live with him. The relief this brings Najaf is palpable. He reads the words with 'a smile … that makes [his] jaw ache' (p.223) and wants to hang a sign on his shop window that says 'Closed due to the happiness of Najaf Mazari' (p.224). This episode evokes the dreadful anxiety asylum seekers endure while governments investigate and make decisions about the granting of refugee status.

Islam

Najaf's faith pervades his perspective and informs his character. Although the narrator does not seek to convert readers to his faith, nor champion it as a faith better than others, his beliefs contribute to the text's key themes, ideas and values. Therefore, a basic understanding of Islam helps the reader better appreciate Najaf's story.

Najaf is a Muslim, a follower of the Islamic faith. Islam is closely related to both Christianity and Judaism. All of these faiths honour only one God, known as 'Allah' in Islam. The core difference between the three religions concerns the significance given to Jesus and other prophets. Muslims believe that Muhammad was the last prophet and that he corrected the errors of Christian and Jewish prophets in understanding the word of God.

Afghanistan is an Islamic country. Approximately 99 per cent of the population is Muslim. But, like Christianity and Judaism, there are many branches or denominations of Islam, each with a different view of how the faith should be interpreted or practised. Islam has two main denominations, Sunni and Shi'a. Sunni is the more populous denomination, with around eighty-five to ninety per cent of Muslims subscribing to it. Najaf, though, is a Shi'a, like most Hazara, which makes him part of a minority in Afghanistan.

While Najaf's faith is strong, he is not a proponent of fundamentalism. All major religions have fundamentalist elements: those interpretations that take the holy book or message therein to be the direct word of God, and who follow and enforce uncompromising rules concerning diet, dress, education, worship and numerous other facets of life. The Taliban is a fundamentalist faction. Najaf is far more liberal and sees religion as something personal rather than something to be forced on others. He comments, 'those who honour other gods than mine – peace to them, forever. Those who honour no God at all – peace to them, too' (p.172). The blind and uncompromising faith of the Taliban is something Najaf cannot comprehend and constitutes one of his major criticisms of them.

GENRE, STRUCTURE & LANGUAGE

Genre

The Rugmaker of Mazar-e-Sharif is an instance of 'life writing', a general term for writing that takes a life as its subject. Both biography (an account of someone's life written by another person) and autobiography (where an author writes about their own life) are types of life writing. Authorship constitutes the key difference between the two genres. Autobiography derives from the Greek words 'autos' (self), 'bios' (life) and 'graphe' (writing), so it literally means 'self life writing', or an author writing about their own life. Biography, without the 'auto' prefix, is simply 'life writing', in which an author writes about another person.

The Rugmaker of Mazar-e-Sharif can be described as either biography or autobiography, depending on whether Najaf or Hillman is regarded as the author. If we view Najaf as the author of *The Rugmaker of Mazar-e-Sharif*, we would describe the text as an autobiography. Conversely, if we regard Hillman as the author, we would class it as biography. In either case, using these simple labels is problematic because we consequently overlook the contribution of either Najaf or Hillman.

'Collaborative autobiography' is perhaps the best way to describe the genre of *The Rugmaker of Mazar-e-Sharif*. Theorists of autobiography often use this term to refer to autobiographical texts that are produced by two or more people. This useful term not only enables us to appreciate the input of both Najaf and Hillman in writing the narrative, but also illuminates the processes by which the narrative was produced. Najaf shared his story with Hillman in a series of meetings and interviews. Hillman, an experienced writer, crafted Najaf's oral story into a unified and engaging written narrative.

Hillman's involvement in Najaf's story does not mean that we should regard *The Rugmaker of Mazar-e-Sharif* as any less factual or reliable than a single-author autobiography. Autobiography is usually classified as nonfiction; readers frequently expect autobiographical writing to be as accurate and factual as newspaper articles or textbooks. But the divide between fiction and nonfiction in autobiographical writing is always blurry. An autobiography is not the author's life as lived, but an imaginative re-creation of certain aspects of that life crafted into narrative. Autobiographers almost always write creatively. They might, for example, rearrange the chronology of events or add a perspective or understanding acquired much later. This is exactly the role Hillman performs in writing *The Rugmaker of Mazar-e-Sharif* with Najaf. By dubbing this text 'collaborative autobiography' we can continue to approach it as autobiography while remaining aware of the roles both authors played in writing it.

The Rugmaker of Mazar-e-Sharif is also an unusual autobiography because it portrays its protagonist (central character) as ordinary. Typically, the subject of an autobiography is constructed as unique or unusually interesting in some way. Najaf, despite his amazing story, is characterised quite differently. In fact, he is positioned as a member of a community. The narrator frequently uses the inclusive, collective pronoun 'we' in preference to the singular 'I'. The narrator's reference to Woomera inmates as 'us', for example, places Najaf within a community. The same pronoun is used, with the same effect, when Najaf recounts his journey on the people-smugglers' boat and when he describes the people of Mazar-e-Sharif nervously awaiting the Taliban's return. This deviation from the conventions of autobiography is important because it contributes to both the text's key themes and to the characterisation of Najaf.

Structure

Najaf's story unfolds through two interlinking narratives: the first detailing his life in Australia from the time of his detainment in Woomera, and the second recounting his life in Afghanistan from boyhood to adulthood. Each narrative frame uses a different tense. The chapters set in Australia are narrated in the present tense and are set in the six-year period from 2001 to 2006, when Najaf is granted Permanent Residency Status and reunited with Hakima and Maria. Those set in Afghanistan use the past tense and cover the period from about 1977 to 2001, the year of Najaf's flight. The two time frames eventually converge: the last chapter in the Afghanistan sequence describes Najaf's journey to Australia. This brings us to the point at which the first Australian chapter, and the text itself, commences.

Importantly, the chapters alternate so that each chapter in the Australian sequence is followed by one from the Afghanistan sequence. This highly effective narrative strategy demonstrates the ways in which Najaf's past informs his present and gives the reader a greater understanding of Najaf's experiences and emotional states when in Australia. For example, when Najaf comments in Woomera that 'for me, the middle of the night is not a good time' (p.156), we know that this fear is a consequence of the traumatic explosion that destroyed his family's home and killed his brother in 1985. Similarly, the description of traditional home-based Afghani rug factories, where the weavers, teachers and apprentices 'chatter and joke and sing' (p.91) contrasts with the industrial carpet factories Najaf later sees in Melbourne. By foregrounding the present and enlisting stories from the past to illuminate that present, the authors focus our attention on Najaf's experience as a refugee. His fears, frustrations, hopes and joys are contextualised and therefore made comprehensible to readers who, perhaps, have never experienced the things Najaf has experienced.

The text also evokes a deeper past than Najaf's own personal one, a past that belongs to the timelessness of tradition. Traditional stories are used to help Najaf understand aspects of his life or to communicate his point of view to the reader. These stories form part of the text's structure. Such stories include the fables of Kandhi Hazara, the extraordinary dancer assassinated by mujahedin troops; of the King's Son and the Canary Birds, which Gorg Ali tells to prepare Najaf for working life; and of the old camel that perseveres up the mountain path without complaint. These stories help us understand Najaf's character, his way of thinking and his beliefs. They also work in tandem with the interweaving time frames to reveal the enormity of the challenges Najaf faces as a refugee. In addition to the fear and pain he suffers during the wars in Afghanistan, and the painful uncertainty of his long wait for permanent residency, Najaf has to negotiate and participate in a culture very different from his own. These fables, and Najaf's reverent attitude towards them, succinctly communicate the vast differences between Anglo-Australian and Afghani culture.

Language

Perhaps one of the most striking features of *The Rugmaker of Mazar-e-Sharif* is the simplicity of its language. The text narrates violent events, depicts complex and powerful emotions and explores weighty themes, yet consistently uses straightforward, unadorned language. For example, when Najaf is captured by the Taliban, he (along with the other 40 men with whom he is imprisoned) hears the screams of men being tortured with whips made of steel cable. This is an extremely violent act and its effect on the witnesses is unimaginably harrowing. That horror is conveyed with simple candour: 'All of us within listened to the screams with our heads bowed. Some men vomited where they stood. Others let their urine flow without shame' (p.201). No description is given, no similes or metaphors are used, but the terror of the moment is starkly conveyed through short, direct sentences.

The same tautness of language is used throughout the text to convey joy as well as terror and tragedy. It is also used to explore questions about the justness and purpose of war: highly complicated ideas reduced, powerfully, to simple questions. 'What can you make with a gun?' Najaf asks. 'Can you make a rug with a gun? Can you build a family with a gun?' (p.52).

Language choice is never incidental. Writers make careful and deliberate decisions about the language they employ because language choice contributes enormously to the tone, structure, thematic direction and integrity of the overall narrative. So it is important to look at what simple language achieves in *The Rugmaker of Mazar-e-Sharif*. First, it conveys character. English is Najaf's second language, and one he only began to speak with any regularity when he arrived in Australia as a thirty-year-old refugee. The unembellished and short sentences used to convey Najaf's voice in text are therefore consistent with his own experience. Second, the language reflects the collaborative process that produced this autobiography. The text reads like spoken language. It is straightforward, direct and succinct. In this way, it echoes how Najaf might have told his story to Hillman in the meetings and interviews the two shared when writing the text. The language, in a sense, rings true as Najaf's voice. Hillman is careful to give Najaf a voice, rather than impose his own way of speaking or writing upon Najaf's story. This is another reason why we can comfortably understand *The Rugmaker of Mazar-e-Sharif* as autobiography, rather than biography.

Further, the simplicity of the language mirrors Najaf's outlook on life. Najaf has simple beliefs. This does not mean that he is naive or guileless, or that he views things as starkly black and white, but that his outlook is unpretentious, humble and sincere. The language used in the text is in harmony with that aspect of Najaf's character, which endows the narrative with integrity and believability.

CHAPTER-BY-CHAPTER ANALYSIS

Singing in the Wilderness (pp.1–6)

Summary: *Najaf, heartsick in Woomera, sings an Afghani love song.*

The image of Najaf wandering around Woomera illustrates his complete separation from home. This is amplified by the strange community within Woomera, composed of 'hundreds of people from lands ... that are ... mysterious' to Najaf (p.1); by the environment that is indefinably different from his homeland; and by the chapter's anonymity. The narrator is not named until the end of the third paragraph.

A series of misunderstandings also illustrates Najaf's displacement. He cannot understand queues. He cannot produce a birth certificate, only a taskera (an Afghan identity card) that documents his family history. When he tries to ease his heartache by singing, the Australian officers cannot comprehend his reluctance to perform the song for an audience.

Key point

The Australians' interest in the song gives Najaf hope. He becomes, in his own mind and in the eyes of the officials, 'a man with something to offer, a song to sing and maybe a tale to tell that might be worth listening to' (p.5). He is also endorsed to the reader as a person whose story is worth reading.

Q How does this chapter set up Najaf's autobiography? What key ideas are introduced?

Fire in the Night (pp.7–17)

Summary: *A rocket explodes above Najaf's house.*

The rocket explosion powerfully illustrates the unjust ways civilians suffer conflict's immediate consequences. Najaf and his family have no faith in war or in the 'grand claims of salvation' made by the parties fighting (p.10). They are neutral civilians, and yet become direct victims. Najaf, his brother and mother are injured. Rosal Ali is killed. Their home is badly damaged.

Najaf also suffers indirectly. He witnesses many explosions, 'always unwillingly' (p.7), and sees people 'turned inside out' and buildings destroyed (p.8). He has grown used to living with fear and apprehension because 'feeling secure was never a long-term thing' in Afghanistan (p.11). Najaf is a spectator, a bystander who has no active part in the fighting, who exercises no choice, but endures its painful consequences.

Q Describe the tone of the second paragraph. How is it achieved? What effect does it have?

Q Najaf gives a very thorough description of his house. Why? What does it contribute to the chapter?

Shoes (pp.18–32)

Summary: *Najaf describes life in Woomera.*

Najaf articulates the powerlessness latent in the preceding chapters. The anxiety of waiting for a decision about his refugee status is made to feel interminable by the fact that the decision rests with distant others.

Najaf responds with hard work. Working in the kitchen provides distraction, as well as an opportunity to prove his worthiness to Australian officials. To Najaf, 'work repays your debt to God for making you a human being' (p.25). This idea, which becomes a narrative motif, is enhanced by Najaf's thorough and proud description of his kitchen work.

Other detainees respond less constructively. Their anxiety generates arguments and violence. In this heated environment, differences are accentuated and the detainees wage 'tiny wars' (p.24). Key elements of Najaf's character are illuminated against this simmering tension. Greeting all inmates and carefully doling out equal food portions illustrate Najaf's respect for everyone and his peaceable nature. His compassion is further demonstrated by his notion that detainment leads to the 'poem each man and each woman and each child carries inside' being forgotten (p.30).

Q Najaf imagines a letter a friend might send to endorse him to the Australian government. What does this imagined letter reveal about Najaf's values? Are these the same things the Australian government will value when making their decision?

Q What causes Woomera's 'tiny wars', in Najaf's opinion? What is his attitude towards these conflicts?

Lambs and Wolves (pp.33–44)

Summary: *Najaf works as a shepherd and goes to school.*

Najaf's description of his boyhood provides an insight into Afghani culture. Aged eight, Najaf shoulders great responsibility in protecting the family flock. Najaf's work is so important that it takes priority over school, which he claims is common, though it might seem strange to an Australian reader today. Najaf's calm response to his father's death might also seem odd, but he explains the differences between Afghani family structures and typical Australian ones.

The sketch of Afghani culture extends beyond Najaf's personal and family experience to include an outline of the country's tumultuous history. A crucial component of this historical analysis is Najaf's description of the zealous fighting ethic of Afghani people, a characteristic Najaf lacks. His historical sketch also demonstrates how entrenched conflict is in Afghanistan.

Key point

Najaf's childhood is portrayed as a time of peace. He describes a kind of paradise: 'the silence ... the mists and clouds and the sunshine and the snow and how bright the grass was in spring' (p.39). But the narrator recognises that this is a trick of memory. Najaf idealises the mountainside as a paradise for two reasons. First, it probably seems idyllic because he comes to have so many terrible experiences. Second, his memory is tinged with nostalgia – a characteristic of many autobiographical narratives which recall a time of childhood innocence, a time often free of the cares and woes of adulthood.

Q Najaf asks, 'how could it help me to know of the great oceans of the world, of the continents, of lands ten thousand miles away that I would never visit?' (p.40). Why could this be described as ironic?

Q Najaf makes 'a great leap through time and over distance' to include an anecdote about Maria's school in Australia (p.43). Why does he make this leap?

The Room of Questions (pp.45–52)

Summary: *Najaf is interviewed by immigration officers.*

The interview exposes cultural differences and shows how these become very significant in certain situations. Najaf very nearly answers the question about the Shrine of Ali unsatisfactorily because he interprets it from his own perspective, rather than from the interviewer's: 'we don't call it famous, because it is too holy to be famous' (p.51). This highlights the precariousness of Najaf's situation, even though he is now safe from war.

Najaf's feelings about the interview also reflect the consequences of conflict. He is apprehensive and suspicious, fearing that an enemy may have fed misinformation to the Australian authorities. He breaks down when questioned about Gorg Ali. Najaf's grief also introduces one of his fundamental objections to conflict. Gorg Ali is described as a special creation of God. His callous death is therefore a travesty. Najaf loathes war not just because of how it has affected him, but also because it contradicts his faith.

Q How is language used to convey tension during the interview?

Q How can you explain Najaf's statement about the 'lie that helps tell the bigger truth' (p.47)?

Kisses (pp.53–67)

Summary: *Najaf moves to Mazar-e-Sharif; the Taliban are introduced.*

Two moves are documented: the Mazaris' move to Mazar-e-Sharif and Najaf's move from childhood to pubescence. Identity is therefore the predominant idea of this chapter.

The attitude to hard work evoked earlier is reiterated and given a religious and cultural significance: 'It is important to Afghanis to feel that what comforts come from God have been earned, and particularly important to the Hazara' (p.54). Najaf then recounts the story of Abdul Ali Mazari, a fierce opponent of the Taliban, who maintained a frugal Hazara lifestyle despite his important position. Najaf's integration of his personal story of building the house with the story of a great leader creates a sense of shared tradition and group identity.

The wedding ceremony has a similar function. Najaf's description foregrounds tradition and the importance of local communities. The ceremony itself celebrates constancy, demonstrated in the mullah's telling 'of the deeds and piety' of 'the groom's father and grandfather and great-grandfather and maybe even great-great-grandfather' (p.58). Cultural persistence is echoed throughout the chapter, often in casual asides such as Najaf's comment that the roofs of Afghani houses have been made in the same way for thousands of years.

Q What is the significance of the story about Kandhi Hazara?

Q 'The dancing of Afghanistan is to belly dancing what a fine feast prepared by a master chef is to a hamburger from the restaurants of McDonald's' (p.60). What does Najaf mean by this? Describe the tone. Why does he use this tone?

School (pp.68–76)

Summary: *Najaf graduates from November to Mike compound.*

Woomera detainees are under constant scrutiny. Najaf wittily describes the surveillance as a series of tests, including the 'Don't-Jump-the-Queue test', the 'Wait-Your-Turn test', and the 'What-Are-You, Some-Sort-of-Gourmet? test' (p.70). Najaf learns as much about Australian culture and expectations from these perceived tests as he does from the formal lectures he attends about 'Australian laws and Australian culture' (p.72).

Najaf's sense of powerlessness remains in spite of his jocular tone. He exercises some agency by refusing to participate in the camp's tacit tests. 'I never really went out of my way to score highly,' he says. 'If I smiled, it was because I felt like smiling' (p.70). Najaf also gains some control over his situation by becoming a mess supervisor and leader of his Afghani group. He enlists the help of an Iranian friend to translate the police officer's lectures for the men in his group and arranges for an Afghani to serve meals to other Afghanis to prevent small grievances erupting into heated arguments or resulting in deportation. Achieving these things, and ensuring peace among his group, leads Najaf to hope and to smile.

Q Najaf says, 'not everyone would see it that way, but to a refugee like me, it looked inhuman' (p.69). How does Najaf's perspective shape this chapter?

Q What do the topics of the police officer's talks suggest about Australian values? How do these sit with Najaf's own values?

The King's Son and the Canary Birds (pp.77–94)

Summary: *Najaf begins his rugmaking apprenticeship.*

It is probably unthinkable to most Australian readers that a twelve-year-old boy would begin full-time work, and that he would continue that work for the rest of his life, so Najaf retells the fable he was told by Gorg Ali when he himself was being prepared for work. The story communicates a number of subtleties. It demonstrates Afghanis' regard for security, sustenance and hard work over luxury and leisure. It evinces (shows) the precariousness of Afghani society. Finally, it shows that women traditionally have a voice in Afghani culture.

Najaf is first employed as a blacksmith's apprentice. He hates the work, largely because he has no opportunity to create beautiful things. When

Sarwah introduces Najaf to rugmaking, he interprets the intervention as a case of good fortune, or a rare opportunity from God. Najaf eagerly takes up the apprenticeship, despite demonstrating the resilience and fortitude expected of an Afghani boy when struggling with the blacksmith's work.

Q How is language used to portray the differences between the blacksmith's shop and the rugmaking factories?

Q Why is creating beautiful things so important to Najaf?

Main Camp (pp.95–104)

Summary: *Najaf moves to Main Camp.*

This chapter is about hope. Knowing that a decision about his future is imminent, Najaf begins to daydream about life in Australia: imagining the car he will drive, the garden he will tend and the shop he will run. Daydreaming is Najaf's way of nurturing hope. Yet he knows hope can be dangerous in Main Camp, where a knock on the door could come at any moment, 'and that knock will mean either great happiness, or the worst unhappiness in the world' (p.96). The misery that bad news can bring is forcefully illustrated by the self-mutilation perpetrated by the Afghani refused asylum in Australia.

Key point

Tension is elevated in Main Camp because the stakes are higher: 'From here, there are only two places you can go: into the land of Australia, or to the country where you came from' (p.95). Inertia and anxiety lead to protest: deliberate actions directed outward towards the Australian officials, unlike the inwardly focused arguments between detainees described previously. Two protests are documented: one that symbolises utter despair (the man sewing his lips together) and another that represents hope (the release of the caged birds).

Q Another fable is shared in this chapter. Why does Najaf remind himself of this story? What does it tells us about Najaf? In what other ways does this chapter evince the value of resilience?

Q Najaf knows if a man is Afghani, 'by the way he walks, by the way he stands ... by his eyes and the way he looks back at me' (p.100). How does this differ from the way Australian authorities might establish identity?

Gorg Ali and the Watermelons (pp.105–19)

Summary: *Gorg Ali is killed.*

Gorg Ali's death is a personal calamity for Najaf and his family. He was an adored son and brother, who capably and sensibly headed the family. But this chapter makes the personal heartbreak something greater. It makes Gorg Ali's death emblematic of the unfairness, futility and tragedy of war.

Gorg Ali is a good, sensible and practical man, 'free of much of the madness that drives other people to do bad things, or things that are bad for the soul' (p.106). He has no faith in fighting, viewing it as futile and destructive. He also embodies the constancy and wisdom of tradition, as his power over snakes illustrates. That such a man is killed by a stray bullet in a skirmish that achieves nothing, his body left among debris in a field, is perhaps the strongest indictment of war made in the text so far.

Q What is the significance of Najaf's argument with Rosal Ali? What elements of Najaf's character are exposed?

Q What is 'the big black cloud' that sits 'right on top' of Najaf's family and neighbours (p.116)?

Love and Music (pp.120–7)

Summary: *Abbas asks for Najaf's help in a love affair.*

This chapter develops the idea that Woomera functions as a community within itself, where friendships are forged, babies are born and people love. It also shows that detainees bring their familiar practices and assumptions with them to continue in a new place. For example, Abbas plays his tula to appreciative crowds. When Najaf goes to speak with

Abbas' love, they hold their conversation in the open because 'it is important that people see that [they] are not attempting a secret meeting' (pp.125–6). The woman rejects Abbas' proposal on the grounds that her two brothers must decide whom she marries.

This touching episode develops Najaf's character. Not only does Abbas trust the honourable Najaf with the sensitive mission, we also see how Najaf tenderly protects his friend: by not revealing his name to the woman, and again by asking the woman not to avoid Abbas, so that his friend's feelings are not hurt. Najaf's respect for people, for their honour and integrity, is evidently deep and genuine.

Q How does Abbas' music affect the refugees who listen? Why do they value his music so much?

Two Red Pills (pp.128–40)

Summary: *Najaf's injured leg causes him great suffering until he is cured by two red pills prescribed by a psychologist.*

The personal costs Najaf experiences in the aftermath of the rocket attack are recounted: the injury to his leg, his inability to work, his subsequent begging and the worry and shame this brings.

Najaf's rehabilitation is a test of his character. He is jealous of boys running on 'two strong legs' (p.134). He wants to shout at the doctor and is rude to the taxi driver who offers help. Uncharacteristically, he is, for a time, 'downcast' and forgets to count his 'blessings' (p.134), worried that 'God had chosen [his] family for special suffering' (p.128).

Najaf's doubts, however, are resolved and this chapter actually works to solidify his beliefs and character. In the months that he cannot work, he does not sulk or wait for a miracle. Instead, he is industrious and pragmatic, knitting and selling woollen socks. His two core values are stated. First, lying idle in hospital, Najaf realises 'that a man is not what he thinks, not what he says, but what he does with his hands and legs and with his heart' (p.132). Second, after the psychologist's mysterious two red pills effect a recovery, Najaf simply accepts that 'God provides' (p.140). Najaf's resilience and faith win out over his doubts.

Q What does Najaf's description of the hospital reveal about the impact of war in Afghanistan?

Q Why does Najaf feel 'sick with shame' (p.137)?

Apple (pp.141–7)

Summary: *Najaf has a bewildering conversation with a young widow.*

This second instance of unrequited love within Woomera demonstrates that 'life is a force that never takes a holiday', even though Woomera's enforced waiting had initially led Najaf to believe that 'life had paused' (p.141). The effect of this idea, developed in various ways throughout the chapter, is to diminish the perceived difference between refugees and the outside community.

Najaf's reverie about the 'Woomerians' rebuilding Australia is important in this context because it dispels some popular myths about refugees. The Woomera population comprises not only desperate and poor people, but also artists, businesspeople, scientists, teachers and religious leaders, as well as the 'scoundrels and thugs and criminals and bullies' (p.142) that exist in any community. As Najaf states, and his encounter with the widow shows, refugees have the same passions and dreams as any other members of the 'human family' (p.142) and the 'new Australia' the Woomerians would build would be shaped by those same passions, needs and interests. They 'would make everything that is here already' (p.142). Woomerians are simply people, too.

Q Najaf uses 'we' to refer to the community within Woomera. Why? What is the effect of using this pronoun?

Q Woomera is described as 'the world packed into a small parcel' (p.142). What examples in this chapter, and in earlier ones, show Woomera as a microcosm of the wider world?

Land of Armies (pp.148–54)

Summary: *Najaf returns to work and dodges army recruiters.*

The peace and contentment Najaf enjoys in his craft are juxtaposed with the precariousness of living in a war zone. He, like other teenage boys, must keep his 'eyes peeled' (p.152) and 'one part' of his brain 'always on alert' (p.153) to avoid recruitment into armed service. Conscripting boys for armed combat was, at that time, a terrible social consequence of Afghanistan's incessant war, illustrated here alongside other such consequences, including the people's loss of faith in political leaders (who 'had forgotten everything about Afghanistan except their desire to rule it', p.150) and economic dependence on war as the country's major industry and employer.

Perhaps the most damaging consequence of persistent conflict, however, is the sense of powerlessness instilled in Afghanis, captured in Najaf's despondence while he works at the loom. Although his work brings him joy, the unremitting war means he must train himself 'not to think too far into the future' (p.154). Najaf resigns himself to the fact that his future depends on things he cannot control.

Q What is conveyed by the simile comparing warring parties to boxers, who fight until one 'would finally fall down dead, but the other would be a cripple for the rest of his life' (p.150)?

The Other Side of the Fence (pp.155–62)

Summary: *Najaf and his friend Nemat are mistakenly told they have received visas. Days later, a visa arrives.*

In Australia, Najaf's fate still sits in the hands of others, this time those of the 'Canberra Australians' whose 'special stamp on a piece of paper' allows an asylum seeker to stay (p.155). Najaf receives false news that a visa has been granted. Najaf's response to this disappointment reveals a key philosophy in his outlook and provides an insight into his ability to persevere. 'We have many more disappointments than days of wonderful news,' says Najaf, 'because we are human beings and we are given a hoping heart by God' (pp.158–9). We cannot live without hope, and it is hope that enables Najaf to go on.

Q How do the authors convey Najaf and Nemat's elation when they first hear that visas have arrived? In what ways does the second scene, when Najaf receives news of the real visa, differ?

Strawberries (pp.163–82)

Summary: *The Taliban rise to power; Najaf marries Hakima.*

In parallel to 'Apple', this chapter illustrates that life carries on in war-torn Afghanistan. Najaf makes modest plans for the future and, after his mother vetoes an early courtship, marries Hakima. The ceremony rebuts the war's immediacy. Najaf feels connected to a 'long, long line of ... ancestors stretching for a great distance' (p.181) and thus enjoys a sense of continuity, despite war's disruptiveness.

Resilience is increasingly important. The conflict has changed in the years leading up to Najaf's marriage. The Soviet Union has been defeated and, as disparate mujahedin forces fight each other, a new party enters the conflict: the Taliban. This chapter sets Najaf's deeply personal story of love and marriage alongside a broad historical outline about the Taliban.

Criticism of the Taliban is rooted in Najaf's own opinions and beliefs. They outlaw many things Najaf has described with great affection and joy: music, singing and dancing. Their refusal to doubt is shown to be dangerous because Najaf holds that doubt is a human attribute given by God. The observation that no Talib 'could stand in wonder and gaze at the beauty of things' is powerful because we know how important appreciation of beauty is to Najaf (p.176). Indeed, it is weaving beautiful rugs while planning family life that enables Najaf to retain high spirits in spite of the war.

Q What point is made by the analogy about 'strawberry' love? What does Najaf's criticism of 'strawberry' love and endorsement of 'bread' (pp.166–7) reveal about Afghani culture?

The Miracle of the Wire Brush (pp.183–91)

Summary: *Najaf begins building a life in Melbourne.*

Like many in the Australian sequence, this chapter charts differences between Afghani and Australian culture. Najaf notices that people in Melbourne walk differently from Afghanis, that they wear different clothes and that they obey traffic lights. The tone is one of mesmerised delight, quite unlike the despondent and confused tone employed in the Woomera chapters.

Najaf also delights in people he meets, such as the greengrocer who generously sells him the wire brushes and the woman who directs him to the Prahran rug shop. Najaf describes these people using language familiar from his description of Gorg Ali: they are the kind of people 'who make the world possible' (p.189). Najaf's encounters with less scrupulous people, such as the two exploitative employers, expose negative attitudes towards refugees. Both employers are from Najaf's 'region of the world', yet treat him as if he 'would endure any sort of treatment just to keep' his job (p.189).

Q What does Najaf's description of Tasmania suggest about his preparedness for life in Australia?

Q What function does hard work have at this point in Najaf's life?

Massacre (pp.192–202)

Summary: *The Taliban invade Mazar-e-Sharif. Najaf hides for 15 days, but is later captured.*

This chapter constitutes the dramatic climax of the text. The narrative, however, retains its characteristic restraint from hyperbole. Dramatic events are narrated using the text's characteristically unembellished (straightforward) language.

As an adult Hazara man, Najaf is now a direct target. It follows that this chapter details how conflict's immediate effects have shaped him. Most notably, Najaf has heightened senses. When the massacre begins, he quickly deduces what is happening because 'the noise of automatic weapons fire was building into a roar, not like the brief bursts you would normally hear' (p.194). Similarly, he is able to distinguish between 'screams of terror' and screams of 'people who had been injured' (p.194). Later, when forced into the Taliban truck, he describes the other Hazara men's expressions as 'those that you see on the faces of all men who have lost any say in whether they live or die' (p.199). Najaf is wise about terrible things.

Q Why does Najaf begin this chapter with the story about lambs and wolves? What does it contribute?

Q What is the significance of the similes likening Najaf to a wild animal?

Shop (pp.203–15)

Summary: *Najaf opens a rug shop and adjusts to Australian life.*

The opening of Najaf's shop demonstrates his successful adjustment to Australian life. This acclimatisation is also indicated in his mastery of the answering machine, which leaves Hakima, still in Pakistan, utterly bewildered, and in his use of a distinctively Australian simile, likening taxation paperwork to St Kilda Beach's pestering seagulls (p.213).

Najaf, though, is still learning, as his amusing negotiations with the bank teller and potential flatmates illustrate. Through Najaf's perspective, we see the faint ridiculousness of student housing, vegetarianism and the bank's EFTPOS policies, and gain an understanding of the challenges Najaf surmounts.

Despite his achievements, Najaf remains anxious. His fate still rests with the Canberra Australians who, having granted him a Temporary

Protection Visa only, can force him to return to Afghanistan at any time. Najaf's comical setting free of canaries and goldfish is a rebellion against his inertia and powerlessness.

Q Najaf likes birds because 'they are intelligent, they work hard to make a living, and they find time to sing' (p.206). Why are these attributes appealing to Najaf? Why else might birds be meaningful to him?

Q What does Najaf's sorrowful question, 'can I ever feel the truth about myself in Australia?' (p.211) suggest about the link between place and identity?

Exile (pp.216–22)

Summary: *Najaf hides from the Taliban in the countryside until his family arranges his escape.*

Najaf's first exile in the countryside is a 'desperate plan' (p.217) and one that is ultimately damaging to the human spirit. Najaf eventually gives up, but more out of self-respect and dignity than frustration or defeat.

A second exile follows. Najaf reluctantly agrees to his family's plan to smuggle him out of Afghanistan. The threat of the Taliban is so great that Najaf flees even though 'it is a terrible thing to turn your face away from your own land' (p.221).

Key point

The explanation of his family's decision demonstrates Najaf's characteristic humility. The decision is not based on favouritism, but on purely practical grounds: he is most in danger, has some knowledge of English and is the most even-tempered of the family. Najaf's humility underpins one of the key ideas of the text: that individual experiences of war are not unique.

Q Why does Najaf move from house to house in Shar Shar? What does this suggest about his character?

Q What is Najaf's attitude towards the Taliban's strictures against women? How does this enlighten us about popular perceptions of Afghanistan?

Home (pp.223–6)

Summary: *Najaf receives Permanent Residency Status.*

Great joy and great sorrow are captured in this chapter. Najaf's belief in hard work and persistence is confirmed by the government's granting of Permanent Residency Status. This decision has two consequences: one, Najaf is finally relieved of the anxiety associated with powerlessness; two, he can be reunited with Hakima and Maria.

Najaf's jubilation, however, is tempered by grief for a friend, a fellow Afghani he met in Australia. Najaf's grief illustrates how important friends have become. Friends such as Ali Sarwari and Robin, his 'second mother' (p.226), have helped Najaf establish the community on which a sense of home is founded.

Q How are Najaf's joy and enthusiasm conveyed?

Journey (pp.227–40)

Summary: *Najaf travels to Australia.*

The dangerous journey illustrates the desperation of Najaf's decision to flee. He entrusts his life to Qadem, a Pashtun (an ethnic group living predominantly in Afghanistan and Pakistan) and traditional enemy. He climbs into a truck apparently filled with Taliban. He boards a boat that 'looked about to fall to pieces and sink' (p.232). Najaf's journey is all the more nerve-racking because he is ignorant about what is happening and where he is going. It is only when he boards an aeroplane bound for Jakarta that Najaf learns his final destination is Australia. This, too, shows the utter desperation of his situation in Afghanistan.

The journey also highlights Najaf's naivety about the wider world. He has never seen a boat or the ocean and, as he comments in Jakarta, never realised that the world outside Afghanistan is 'truly real' (p.231). In part, this is due to his scant formal education; but arguably it also results from his almost constant experience of conflict. For much of his life, Najaf is preoccupied with simply surviving. It is difficult to imagine he would have the time or inclination to learn about the distant world.

Q Najaf describes the group of refugees as a 'small tribe' (p.231) and again uses inclusive pronouns ('us' and 'we'). What common experiences do the refugees share? Why do they bond together?

Q What is Najaf's attitude towards the boat captain? What is revealed about 'people smugglers' and asylum seekers' relationships with them?

Impossible Things (pp.241–8)

Summary: *Najaf is reunited with Hakima and Maria.*

Settled into a safe life and about to be reunited with Hakima and Maria, certain things seem impossible to Najaf. He now finds it difficult to believe that he hid from the Taliban in a cupboard, or that he travelled so many thousands of kilometres from Afghanistan to Australia. These are 'impossible things'. Najaf has also achieved apparently impossible things. For example, he owns a business, has learnt English, and has established a 'comfortable and clean' home (p.242). The chapter concludes with Najaf's joyful reunion with Hakima and Maria: a thing that seemed so unlikely in Woomera that Najaf could not let himself dream of it.

Q What is the significance of Najaf's final comment, 'What are we waiting for?' (p.248)?

Q How is language used to express Najaf's nervousness?

Postscript (pp.249–53)

Summary: *Najaf reflects upon the anomalies of his new life.*

Some very complex ideas are articulated in this postscript. The two most significant are Najaf's sense of two homes (Australia and Afghanistan) and his attempts to reconcile 'the problem of [his] good fortune' (p.253). Najaf hints that these are issues he will always grapple with, but also suggests that the solution lies in acknowledging the sadness as well as the happiness of his life.

Key point

Najaf points out that people who read his story in the newspaper probably doubted its truthfulness. He imagines the reader asking, 'Could a man who has run for his life leaping the bodies of the dead smile in this way? Surely not!' (p.252). This observation succinctly illustrates the power people have to overcome great adversity, but it also exposes a negative attitude towards refugees. Refugees' claims are often doubted because their stories seem so extraordinary. At this point, we are challenged to consider our own reading of Najaf's story.

CHARACTERS & RELATIONSHIPS

Najaf Mazari

Key quotes

'War had always been the background to my life (and sometimes much more than background) and it surely helped to form the way I thought about things.' (p.163)

'... I realised that a man is not what he thinks, not what he says, but what he does with his hands and legs and with his heart.' (p.132)

'For I like peace. It is part of me, something that was inside of my brain and my heart when my mother gave birth to me.' (p.76)

To Najaf, everything comes back to God because He is 'the One who fashions fortune with His mind and His hands' (p.250). It is important to understand and accept Najaf's faith, even if we hold other opinions, because it is so fundamental to his character. Najaf's faith endows him with resilience and humility and underpins his core values, such as hard work, hope and the freedom to act within his own power. Najaf understands his faith as something deeply personal. While faith informs his identity, Najaf rebukes the Australian assumption that simply labelling him 'Muslim' explains who he is. As he explains, 'if you put ten Muslims together, you have ten different ways of being a Muslim' (p.212). He abhors the notion of fighting on the basis of religion and, being a man of peace, states that he could 'never even raise a feather cushion against another man because of his religion' (p.172).

Najaf's values and character are also inescapably shaped by something that runs utterly counter to his faith: conflict. As he states, war has always been the background to Najaf's life and consequently informs the way he thinks. His distrust of anger and argument as means of resolving problems arises from this backdrop. His resilience, the ability he has to put one foot in front of the other and keep on going, is equally a consequence of his surviving tragedy after tragedy in war as it is of his faith. Similarly, he values hope and autonomy so highly because he has seen the damage the absence of these can inflict on human beings. One of the most significant aspects of Najaf's character is that, despite what he has seen and suffered in his encounters with conflict, he remains hopeful, kind and filled with joy and good humour. Najaf's character demonstrates that people can survive conflict not only physically, but also psychologically.

In discussing Najaf's character, it is always important to be aware of the complexity of a protagonist (main character) in autobiography. Najaf the protagonist is not synonymous (one and the same) with the narrator. As readers of autobiography, it is important for us to distinguish between the protagonist and the narrator, even though this is sometimes very difficult. It is particularly important in reading *The Rugmaker of Mazar-e-Sharif* because the protagonist, Najaf, evolves from a very young village boy living in rural Afghanistan to a thirty-two-year-old refugee supporting a family and running a business in Melbourne. Enormous changes occur in Najaf's life, so we need to pay careful attention to which Najaf is speaking at any point in the narrative. This enables us to see, perhaps more easily than in fiction, how the protagonist's perspective at a given age or in a particular situation informs his interpretation of events and characters.

Gorg Ali

Key quotes

'My brother Gorg Ali ... was one of those people who make the world possible. What I mean is that he was the sort of human being who holds things together, and the opposite of the sort who wrenches things apart.' (p.105)

'He was a peaceful man right down to his bones.' (p.110)

'To make a good man, God has to use all of his skill. Some of the goodness of God himself goes into such a man.' (p.51)

Gorg Ali is elevated to hero status in the narrative. He has a renowned and extraordinary power over snakes, is honoured by the villagers of Shar Shar and, according to Najaf, would have been 'the wise man of the village' or 'even a chieftain' on account of his wisdom and powers had he been born centuries earlier (p.110). Najaf's portrayal of Gorg Ali is at times so laudatory that he feels it necessary to point out he does not 'mean to ask those reading this story to believe that Gorg Ali was a god, or not truly a human being' (p.106).

Numerous factors underpin Najaf's veneration of Gorg Ali. First, and quite simply, Gorg Ali is Najaf's older brother. He admires Gorg Ali in the same way many boys look up to their older brothers. For Najaf, this fairly typical fraternal adulation is compounded by Gorg Ali's position as head of the Mazari family. Being raised by gentle Gorg Ali is something Najaf describes as a 'special good fortune' (p.37). Second, Najaf admires Gorg Ali because he is a good man. Calm, gentle and generous, Gorg Ali is simply commendable. Third, Gorg Ali is idealised and idolised to an even greater degree as a result of his death. Najaf still grieves for his beloved older brother, as is illustrated by the tears he sheds when asked about Gorg Ali during the interview in Woomera.

During the interview, Najaf remembers Gorg Ali 'standing beside me with his hand on my shoulder, me only a small boy' (p.51), which suggests that Najaf remembers Gorg Ali as a father figure. The same sentiment is evident in Gorg Ali's arrangement of Najaf's apprenticeship. Gorg Ali is portrayed here as companionable and compassionate, genuinely concerned about Najaf's happiness. However, this passage belies Najaf's idealisation of Gorg Ali. When Najaf complains about his work, Gorg Ali exclaims, 'I work hard too. Do you hear me crying about it?' (p.84). The narrator presumes 'probably he was disappointed that my job didn't satisfy me' (p.84), but this is a retrospective interpretation. It is equally as plausible that Gorg Ali was angry with his whingeing little brother. The use of one word – 'probably' – shows that Najaf wants to see only the best aspects of Gorg Ali.

Key point

Najaf is only thirteen when Gorg Ali is killed. The portrayal of his character within the narrative is coloured by Najaf's consequent idealisation of his eldest brother.

Frequent symmetry between Najaf's beliefs and ideas and those of Gorg Ali shows that Najaf emulates his idolised older brother. For example, Najaf says Gorg Ali 'could see how easily people argued themselves into a situation that could only end with guns being loaded and knives being drawn' (p.11). In Woomera, Najaf laments that asylum seekers could be 'sent back to Kabul' because of an angry argument over 'a spoonful of rice and half a potato' (p.75). Gorg Ali is described as peaceful 'right down to his bones' (p.110) and Najaf sees peace as an integral part of his own self: 'something that was inside … when my mother gave birth to me' (p.76). Gorg Ali warns his younger brothers to 'steer clear of all political parties, all political disputes' (p.10), advice that Najaf both adopts and integrates into his own beliefs, evident in his comments about having 'no powerful feelings' about either the mujahedin or the communists, only that 'I wanted them to leave me alone' (p.150). Najaf and Gorg Ali's common views explain, to some extent, why the narrator so admires his older brother.

The character of Gorg Ali performs another function in the text. He is instrumental in the authors' indictment of armed conflict. As a man who has an inexplicable power over snakes and who tends the bees that have lived in the hives at Shar Shar for many, many years, Gorg Ali embodies tradition. He represents wisdom, peace and the timelessness of Afghani peasant life. This makes his sudden and pointless death tragic – even more so because neither the Soviets nor the mujahedin accomplish anything in the three-week affray that claims his life.

Abdul Ali

Key quotes

'Abdul Ali didn't have the gentle manner of Gorg Ali … and it was unusual for him to show me affection …' (p.91)

'Was it not possible for my brother to simply ask me for an explanation without boxing my ears? Truly, that was something like the way of the Taliban – first, punish, don't bother about explanations.' (p.94)

Abdul Ali is not portrayed with the same adulation or attention as Gorg Ali. While Gorg Ali features frequently in the narrative despite his death in 1984, Abdul Ali only enters the narrative when he is a participant in an event that the narrator recounts. Additionally, he is depicted as Gorg Ali's opposite: rash where Gorg Ali is patient, violent where Gorg Ali is gentle and angry where Gorg Ali is calm.

This disparity in characterisation is most evident in Najaf's account of his apprenticeship. Here, Gorg Ali is portrayed as gentle and understanding, even where, as suggested above, his words imply other emotions. Abdul Ali, in contrast, is rendered as an impulsively violent man, particularly in the key scene in which he gives the young Najaf 'a mighty blow' for lying about his work (p.93). Najaf accuses Abdul Ali of acting in the 'way of the Taliban' for the summary and ill-considered punishment he inflicts (p.94).

Given what Najaf has said of the Taliban, this comparison implies that Abdul Ali is extremely cruel. But, as with the characterisation of Gorg Ali, it is important to consider the perspective from which Najaf depicts his brother. Najaf is remembering an episode from his childhood, and so his description of it is tinged with the resentment he felt when it occurred. This resentment is accentuated by Najaf's objection to being treated like a child at a time when he is submitting to the responsibilities of working life. Notice the subtle difference between Gorg Ali's conversation with Najaf where the two sit companionably side by side, and Abdul Ali's calling Najaf to the table and dubbing him 'little one' before interrogating him about working at the blacksmith's (p.92). If we consider Najaf's situation objectively, we might interpret Abdul Ali differently. The young Najaf has been lying to his family for weeks, pretending to go to work for Hallim but in fact disappearing to the rug factory. When Abdul Ali confronts Najaf, the boy lies. Abdul Ali's anger does not seem so rash if we view the brothers' exchange from this perspective.

The narrator does evince a more sympathetic attitude towards Abdul Ali later in the text, incidentally, when Najaf is about two years older. Najaf recalls his shame at begging 'a few coins' (p.137) from his brother to pay for the 'medicines and clothes' (p.136) that Najaf cannot afford on the meagre income he makes selling socks. This mortification results not only from Najaf's pride, but also from his sorrow for increasing his brother's financial strain. Najaf's outline of Abdul Ali's expensive responsibilities both helps the reader understand Najaf's chagrin and conveys the narrator's compassion and respect for his brother.

Rosal Ali

Key quotes

'But Rosal Ali would shrug and smile and go on his way, happy to have made me angry, as if that was his great project in life.' (p.85)

'I would not have the chance now to be proud of him. It hurt me deeply to know this.' (p.17)

Rosal Ali, Najaf's younger brother, features in the narrative even less than Abdul Ali. However, he has an important function. Rosal Ali brings out those elements of Najaf's nature that are otherwise concealed. Rage and resorting to violence to express that rage are exhibited only once by Najaf in the text – in his angry argument with Rosal Ali. Najaf, uncharacteristically, hurls abuse at his little brother, using insults such as 'God Himself looks down on you with disgust' and 'He wonders why He made you to begin with' (p.118). Rosal Ali's impudent escape to a locked room incenses Najaf further, to the point that he loses the wisdom he values so much and smashes his fist through a window to grab at his younger brother. The episode shows us that Najaf is not immune to the senseless anger he criticises in others.

Rosal Ali is the antithesis to Najaf's sense of responsibility. At ten years of age, Rosal Ali commences work as a carpenter's apprentice, but Najaf recollects it was 'common for him to simply forget that he had a job at all and stroll off into the city to amuse himself' (p.118). We can understand Najaf's frustration, and the narrator himself recognises that his anger with Rosal Ali is 'to do with the freedom he gave himself' when Najaf's own freedom 'was fading away to nothing' (p.85).

Key point

Characterisation in *The Rugmaker of Mazar-e-Sharif* is dependent on Najaf's perspective. We only ever see characters through Najaf's eyes, and our view of those characters changes as Najaf's interpretations alter in different situations. This limited perspective is unavoidable in autobiographical writing because the narrative is always filtered through the protagonist's point of view.

Rosal Ali's irresponsibility tells us something more about Najaf. The narrator's comments about life for young boys in Afghanistan – for example, that 'almost every boy in Afghanistan ... knows how to make mud bricks' (p.55), and that as 'a small boy' Najaf 'knew one thing above all others: that my life would be a life of work' (p.130) – suggest that Najaf's youthful diligence and conscientiousness is nothing uncommon, but simply the way young Afghani boys are. Rosal Ali's indifference to work, however, demonstrates that this is not the case. Comparing the two youngest Mazari boys illuminates Najaf's soberness as a personal attribute, rather than a general cultural trait.

Najaf's mother

Key quote

'My mother was letting me believe that it was my choice if I married Hakima? There was no way in the world it would be left to my choice unless my mother already knew of Iajaz's sister and approved.' (p.180)

Like Rosal Ali, Najaf's mother is largely a background character who serves an important purpose. Characterisation of Najaf's mother helps dispel some popular generalisations about women in Afghani culture. When Najaf first plans to marry at twenty-one, he immediately seeks the permission of his mother, as custom prescribes. When she flatly denies permission, Najaf accepts her determination without question. The command she has over her sons is similarly demonstrated in the scene where Abdul Ali strikes Najaf. Their mother tells Abdul Ali to let Najaf speak. Despite his rash temper, Abdul Ali immediately obeys and Najaf is 'permitted to sit upright once more and explain' (p.93).

Najaf's mother's authority is conveyed subtly, but Najaf does give the issue full voice in the narrative by stating, 'I must tell you that within Afghani families, women are not powerless. They are not puppets made to do this and that and the other, whether it suits them or not' (p.53).

Hakima and Maria

Key quotes

'[F]or me, for most men of Afghanistan, a wife is the bread of our life. In every land, bread is honoured and thanks given to God for its appearance on the table.' (p.167)

'[A] cloud of sadness made its home over my head for a time ... But when I saw my daughter shining like the sun, the cloud sped away.' (p.253)

Najaf's relationship with Hakima demonstrates the esteem in which women are held in Afghani culture. Hakima never speaks in the text, but there is no doubt that the narrator loves and respects his wife. On his wedding day, Najaf feels blessed with a new kind of happiness, one that makes him feel 'that our lives are important' (p.182), an open defiance of the powerlessness and insecurity associated with living in the midst of conflict. In Woomera, thoughts of Hakima and Maria sustain Najaf through times of excruciating boredom and bleakness, though thinking of them often fills him with sorrow. His nervous preparations while waiting for Colin to drive him to the airport touchingly illustrate Najaf's care for them.

The characterisation of Hakima as an individual is perhaps less important than the way in which she is represented as a wife. Najaf loves Hakima not for her beauty or talents or character traits, the stuff of 'strawberry' love, but because she will nourish him throughout his life. The analogy of 'strawberry love' and 'bread' evokes the deep respect and gratitude Najaf, and men like him, have for women. Understanding this analogy as illustrative of the Hazaras' reverence for women is supported by a criticism Najaf later makes of the Taliban. Upon returning to Shar Shar, Najaf is devastated to see the severe rules the Taliban have enforced upon village women. Najaf's Hazara do not abide this treatment of women, as Najaf makes clear with the maxim: 'We say this about our women: an uneducated father is a pity, but an ignorant mother is a tragedy' (p.219).

Robin and Colin

Key quotes

'If I had known that at the end of my journey, I would find such a friend as Robin, I would have thought all the pain and fear was worthwhile for such a reward.' (p.215)

'[Colin] is a very reliable friend ... His advice to me on business, on life, always goes straight to my heart.' (p.241)

Robin and Colin are Najaf's two closest friends in Australia. They demonstrate the goodness and kindness of people Najaf meets in his new home. Through writing about them, the narrator demonstrates how important friends are in developing a sense of home. Their generosity and willingness to take 'a path to kindness' (p.189) are also important in tempering Najaf's complaints about Woomera and the latent criticisms of Australia's refugee policy that these complaints incorporate.

Najaf's relationships with Robin and Colin are also important in demonstrating how well he adjusts to Australian life. The party Robin holds to celebrate Najaf's citizenship is 'crowded with people' (p.252). Colin is one of 'many, many friends' Najaf has in the rug business (p.241). Perhaps more illustrative of Najaf's cultural acclimatisation is his easy conversation with the vernacular-speaking Colin. That Najaf, a man so steeped in traditional Afghani culture, develops a strong friendship with a character so overtly 'Australian' shows that kindness and respect help people overcome the divisions of cultural difference.

THEMES, IDEAS & VALUES

Encountering conflict

Key quotes

'It is not that Afghanis have chosen a path of suffering out of madness; no, other people have chosen that path for us.' (p.105)

'Could God have intended this? No, he did not intend it. He watches now with even greater sadness in His heart than I have in mine. He must be thinking, "See what I have provided! Soil and sunlight, pastures, mountains, rivers, trees, grain and fruit. And of this paradise, these people have made Hell."' (p.197)

'A gun has one purpose, and that purpose will not build anything, but will only tear down what others have built.' (p.52)

The Rugmaker of Mazar-e-Sharif is Najaf's memoir about encountering and enduring decades of armed conflict in Afghanistan. His insights and ideas about war therefore comprise some of the key themes of the text. The broad theme of 'encountering conflict' can be broken down into at least four sub-themes that are presented, developed and explored in the text.

Key point

Najaf experiences and understands conflict as a civilian, not as someone directly involved in the fighting. A non-combatant is likely to have very different experiences and attitudes about war than would a soldier. Najaf's beliefs and ideas about war result from and reflect his civilian's perspective.

Conflict has far-reaching consequences

The text articulates the many and varied ways conflict affects individuals and communities. The immediate and personal costs of war are often obvious. Gorg Ali and Rosal Ali are killed. Najaf is injured when a bomb explodes above his house and he suffers financial hardship and shame as a result of this injury. Ultimately, Najaf is forced to flee Afghanistan when the Taliban take control of Mazar-e-Sharif.

The text captures the long-lasting emotional trauma that accompanies these violent events. Consider Najaf's emotional state while recovering from his injured leg. He is uncharacteristically despondent, angry and jealous. His inability to contribute to the family income and, worse, calling on his brother's charity, make him feel 'sick with shame' (p.137). While these feelings subside when Najaf is finally cured, other key incidents show that single events have lifelong ramifications. Najaf's grief for Gorg Ali, for instance, does not diminish and he sheds disconsolate tears in the interview at Woomera eighteen years later. Najaf's mother, too, endures lifelong grief. Just before the rocket attack, Najaf comments, 'her heart was still broken after the death of Gorg Ali a year before, and would stay broken for the rest of her life' (p.13).

Long-term consequences of conflict also arise indirectly. Living with conflict makes Najaf perpetually fearful. He is so accustomed to being threatened that he worries, baselessly, that the Australian authorities have been fed misinformation. To avoid forcible recruitment into either the communist or mujahedin forces, Najaf has to keep his 'eyes peeled' and 'one part of [his] brain ... always on alert' (pp.152–3). He is tense, vigilant and constantly 'ready to respond' to seemingly imperceptible signals (p.153). Najaf's safety and security are constantly undermined.

Insecurity leads to a sense of powerlessness. Najaf sums up this state of mind when he realises, early in his rugmaking apprenticeship, that 'this future of learning and gaining greater and greater skill all depended on things that I couldn't control' (p.154). To cope, Najaf trains himself 'not to think too far into the future' (p.154). This demonstrates a terrible and often hidden consequence of war: people lose hope.

Living with war, therefore, changes how Najaf thinks. It also changes how he acts. Simile and metaphor suggest that Najaf develops the instincts of a keenly aware animal. For example, while hiding in the cupboard at Ashraf's house, Najaf and Gassem eat 'in the way that wild animals eat, with our ears pricked for the sound of our enemies' (p.197). Later, as he cycles around the countryside avoiding the Taliban, Najaf is 'always as wary as a wild animal', easily woken by a 'stone rolling down a slope half a kilometre away', or by 'the crack of a twig falling from a tree' (p.218).

Najaf's account also reveals conflict's impact on communities and cultures. Sometimes the narrator simply reports facts to demonstrate this idea. He states, for instance, that life expectancy declined between 1979 and 1999 due to the number of civilian casualties in the successive wars (p.33). He later observes that war is 'the main industry and the biggest employer' in Afghanistan (p.153). At other times, the narrator is more suggestive than explicit. For example, Najaf explains that Afghani fathers parent their sons with 'tough love' to ensure boys can endure the hardship that has been 'the pattern of life' in Afghanistan for 'thousands of years' (p.34). This implies that conflict has shaped Afghani culture. Conflict also shapes other cultural practices. Ashraf's house with the concealed cupboard, for example, suggests that conflict influences housing and architecture.

Conflict is futile and unfair

Najaf sees war after war tear apart Afghanistan and its people. Najaf expects that his country will 'be at war for a long time to come' and notes that peace is not known in Afghanistan (p.251). The best Afghanis hope for is a 'type of balance' between warring factions, a respite from fighting that is 'not exactly peace, and ... not exactly war' (p.116). It is not surprising that Najaf's memoir argues that war is futile.

A number of narrative devices are used to develop this argument. First, the narrator's analysis of broad historical events illustrates the failure of conflict to achieve positive outcomes in Afghanistan. The five successive wars in the narrative's background suggest that conflict only leads to more fighting so that it seems to Najaf 'as if the two sides could fight until not a single building was left standing in the entire country' (p.150). Soldiers demonstrably lose sight of war's political agenda: they do not conscript teenagers who believe in the cause, but care only that the youths can 'carry a gun and shoot people on the other side' (p.151). War in Afghanistan is self-perpetuating. The ultimate outcome of the prolonged conflict is the Taliban, who emerged from poor, fundamentalist refugee communities in India and Pakistan.

Second, Najaf's personal encounters with conflict show it to be ineffectual. Neither the Soviet Union nor the mujahedin accomplish anything in the three-week affray that claims Gorg Ali's life. In Woomera, Najaf sees detainees refused visas or relegated to high-security Sierra because they have been fighting. In Afghanistan, he knows men 'who would be prepared … to commit themselves and a hundred generations of their family to battle, from now until the end of the world' (p.36).

Third, the narrator directly comments on conflict's futility. Najaf frequently states that conflict arises from a lack of common sense, from losing 'all sight of the bigger picture' (p.75), or from 'the passion and anger in the arguments of one political party [that] simply aroused the same sort of passion and anger in another' (pp.10–11). When conflict does arise, it does not offer anything constructive. As Najaf puts it, 'a gun has one purpose, and that purpose will not build anything, but will only tear down what others have built' (p.52). Collectively, these statements help develop the argument that war achieves nothing.

That war is ineffectual as a means of achieving positive social change makes its enormous costs on ordinary people seem acutely unfair. A key idea in demonstrating the unfairness of war is that Najaf's encounters with conflict result from chance, not choice. The narrator evokes this sentiment frequently. For example, in introducing his most calamitous encounter with conflict – the mortar attack on his home – a very simple statement is used to construct Najaf as a spectator: 'I have witnessed a number of explosions in my lifetime, always unwillingly' (p.7). This notion becomes a recurrent motif to describe both Najaf's situation and that of Afghani people in general. The sketch of Afghanistan's history provided by the narrator shows how the country has been repeatedly invaded by various international forces and treated as a pawn 'to fit into the political strategies of the powerful' (p.35). The narrator later remarks on how many heartbreaking stories can be told by ordinary people in Afghanistan and concludes, 'other people have chosen that path for us' (p.105).

The sentiment of these statements is supported by key narrative events. The mortar explosion above Najaf's family home, for example, demonstrates chance. Najaf and his family are not military targets yet the bombs explode on their home. The event is so chaotic and unpredictable that the family does not even know the provenance of the rocket. When a passer-by quizzes the injured Najaf if the rocket was Russian, Najaf can only reply, 'Who knows? We think it was mujahedin' (p.134).

The mortar explosion also demonstrates the callousness with which civilians are treated during this period of conflict. International laws exist to protect civilians during combat, but these were not observed in Afghanistan, according to Najaf's narrative. Of the civil war, the narrator remarks, 'both sides expected that it would be necessary to kill civilians, or at least that it would be too troublesome to avoid killing them' (p.12). The reckless and unconscionable actions of all armies in Afghanistan's recent conflicts are borne out in narrative events: Najaf's house is bombed; Gorg Ali is killed; Hazara men, women and children are massacred in the streets of Mazar-e-Sharif.

Conflict contradicts humanity

Najaf's loathing of conflict arises, in part, from his devout faith. He sees wonder and beauty in the smallest and simplest of things, such as bread and apples, and works diligently to create beautiful things, like his rugs, his family, and a new, safe life in Australia. Armed conflict by its very nature destroys things.

The disparity between war and Najaf's world view is evident in the passage that describes Gorg Ali's death. Gorg Ali is the embodiment of patience, gentleness and good sense, and represents wisdom, peace and the timelessness of Afghani peasant life. Najaf portrays his eldest brother as a man who has 'some of the goodness of God himself' inside of him (p.51). His sudden and meaningless death is therefore tragic. The setting of this episode is also significant in developing the idea that war is unholy. Consider how the field is described. It is an idyll, where poppies, tulips and violets bloom like 'a carpet of coloured snow', where the streams are silver and where the sky is 'so blue that it makes you think, "Yes, that is where Heaven must be"' (p.111). When the soldiers leave, the idyllic landscape is scarred – dotted with shell craters and destroyed buildings, the grass blackened and littered with 'the wrappers of food rations that the Russians had thrown away' (p.114).

The depiction of Gorg Ali's death shows that war destroys what is good and beautiful. The text also argues that, for war to be fought, combatants must blind themselves to the beauty of ordinary things. People must be brutal to kill. This idea is illustrated by the fable about Kandhi Hazara. After the first two mujahedin assassins fail, the third group of soldiers is given strict orders to shoot Kandhi Hazara immediately, without even looking at her. They must literally blind themselves to Kandhi Hazara's beauty in order to kill her. The Taliban, the text suggests, are similarly blind to the beauty of life because they are 'fanatics, without any concern for anything other than fighting or worship' (pp.171–2).

People can survive conflict

While the text vividly illustrates the consequences of war and the immense human suffering it causes, it also shows that individuals and communities can survive conflict, both physically and psychologically. Najaf's arrival in Australia and establishment of a new life in Melbourne is one example of surviving conflict. The text contains many others.

Najaf's comments about ordinary life in Afghanistan testify to the resilience of Afghani civilians. He observes that 'they made plans for the future. They married. They had children. They built houses' (p.164). Najaf himself builds a house, marries and starts a family despite the conflict. Persistence is a recurrent idea. For example, after the death of Gorg Ali, Najaf's family experiences a 'big black cloud' of grief and fear, but they persevere because, as the narrator states, 'in such situations, you must go on working steadily' (pp.116–7). Similarly, after the initial defeat of the Taliban in Mazar-e-Sharif, Najaf and his neighbours go on 'as if the day when the Taliban would return was a long way off' (p.177). The importance of resilience is also expounded in the story of the old camel climbing the mountain path, a tale that is woven into Najaf's own story (p.159).

Characterisation also shows how people survive conflict. Najaf is born into and grew up amidst incessant violence and tragedy, but he is not hardened or made vengeful by this. Rather, he is a sympathetic and compassionate man, who claims that peace 'is part of me' (p.76). Najaf's actions support his description of himself. At Woomera, for instance, he smiles at all the other detainees at breakfast (p.20), carefully serves equal portions of rice and potato to prevent a fight breaking out (p.75), and discreetly protects Abbas' feelings after his marriage proposal is rejected (p.127). Despite his experience of conflict, Najaf remains a demonstrably peaceful and gentle man.

Qadem is another important character in developing this theme. When Najaf discovers that Qadem is in charge of smuggling him out of Afghanistan, he is slightly apprehensive. Qadem is Pashtun, a member of an ethnic group traditionally hostile to Najaf's Hazara. The Taliban, Najaf notes, are mostly Pashtun. But he entrusts his life to Qadem despite his uneasiness, and Qadem conveys him to safety. In the end, it is not that Qadem is Pashtun that matters, but that Qadem knew Najaf:

> We were not strangers. He knew that I worked as a rugmaker, he knew that my family was not involved in fighting the Taliban ... and he knew, too, that I would surely be killed if I remained in Afghanistan. (p.227)

Qadem's actions demonstrate that people can retain their humanity during war and that individuals are not necessarily hardened or brutalised by their encounters with conflict.

Hard work

Key quote

> 'Work repays your debt to God for making you a human being.' (p.25)

Several assumptions underpin Najaf's esteem for hard work. First, Najaf believes that hard work endows a person with ownership and rights, demonstrated in his youthful understanding that his participation in building the family's new home at Mazar-e-Sharif was fundamental to earning 'the right to call this place my home' (p.54). God's gifts, says Najaf, must be earned. This explains why he remains resolute that hard work will earn him a place in Australia. When Najaf imagines the letters of recommendation friends might write to the Canberra Australians, the main testimony he thinks these should convey is that he knows 'how to earn a living' (p.19).

Second, Najaf understands work as a means of worship, a way of thanking God for the gifts he has bestowed. We see this when he discovers rugmaking through the fortuitous intervention of his village friend Sarwah. Najaf reflects that 'God had placed Sarwah in my path … It was now my task to show thanks with hard work' (pp.89–90). Finally, Najaf believes that the worthwhile things in life are built with patience, concentration and joy, because this is how God creates things. This is an assumption he shares with Gorg Ali, who unwaveringly believes that 'things made by sweat and toil were important; things made by lying on a sofa all day long were not' (p.106).

These assumptions about the spiritual nature of hard work help illuminate two important aspects of Najaf's character: his categorical objection to conflict and his astonishing resilience. Najaf cannot abide or understand conflict because it summarily destroys what God has created and what others have built. The destructiveness that is inseparable from war is antithetical to Najaf's belief that the path to happiness is found by working and building. That Najaf finds respite from terror and grief in his weaving, in hard work that achieves something beautiful, is not because his work provides a distraction. To Najaf, hard work is an affirmation of life and faith and a defiance of conflict's iniquities.

Freedom

Key quote

> 'The feeling of having no power to make things happen gets into your heart and you begin to question whether you are really a human being …' (p.71)

Afghanistan's incessant conflict restricts ordinary people's ability to live their lives. Consequently, Najaf holds freedom in high esteem and his narrative explicates the importance of freedom to human beings.

Here, freedom does not mean emancipation from captivity or slavery or imprisonment, but rather autonomy, or the capacity to live and act without undue hindrance.

The value of freedom is predominantly presented through powerful elucidation of its opposite: powerlessness. 'To place your fate in the hands of other people,' says Najaf, 'is never a happy situation' (p.19). Najaf endures this unhappiness for much of his life. In Afghanistan, conflict robs Najaf of security. He has to dodge mujahedin and communist recruiters, worries that another rocket will fall on his home and resigns himself to the sorry realisation that the future he dreams of 'depended on things that I couldn't control' (p.154). The narrator expands this sense of subjection to the country as a whole in the wry passage describing Afghanistan as an 'explosion laboratory' and detailing Afghanis' 'undesired honour of being among the first human beings on earth to be blown to pieces' by 'state-of-the-art Russian weaponry' and America's 'ultra-modern high explosives' (pp.7–8).

But it is in Woomera that Najaf faces the harshest consequences of powerlessness. Constant scrutiny and anxiety affect detainees deeply. Najaf notes that 'you start to think, "Have I lost something that used to be part of me?"' (p.71). Frustrated by their impotence, detainees in Woomera are 'very tense' and 'begin to go mad' (p.74). They can easily become so incensed by something as otherwise trivial as a full plate of food that they risk being sent back to Afghanistan, Chechnya or Iran (p.75). Behind the 'big fences' of Woomera, 'good sense begins to starve to death' (p.29).

Autonomy is shown to be an essential element of a person's humanity. Without power, a person is not quite whole. The text demonstrates that, eventually, a repressed person's soul will rebel. This is what Najaf experiences when he gives up his sanctuary from the Taliban in Ashraf's cupboard, and again when he quits his exile in the countryside around Shar Shar. At this point, the narrator explains that 'the soul reaches a stage when it rebels and cries out to you, "Enough! You are a human being!"' (p.218). It is this desperation that underpins the dual protests in

Woomera. It also explains Najaf's comical releasing of canaries and 'visa fish' (p.207). These entertaining acts are, in this context, not juvenile or frivolous; they demonstrate Najaf's rebellion against the subjection he endures while waiting for the Canberra Australians to make a decision about his visa.

Hope

Key quote

> 'We have many more disappointments than days of wonderful news because we are human beings and we are given a hoping heart by God. If God did not give us the power to hope, we would not have lasted long on His earth.' (pp.158–9)

Hope is a corollary to the despair of powerlessness. Najaf values hope because it gives him strength in the most difficult circumstances. Hope, according to Najaf, is a gift from God that allows people to find the resilience they need to survive in the world. Hope itself is resilient, likened to the 'red flowers around the mosque at Mazar-e-Sharif' that 'bloom each year, no matter how many rockets explode over them' (p.6). But hope also needs to be nurtured. Najaf witnesses hopelessness in Woomera, and its effects are as dangerous and devastating as powerlessness. Without hope, detainees can become ghosts who 'sit on their beds and stare at nothing. When you look into their eyes, you see only emptiness, like a room from which all the furniture has been removed' (p.30).

Najaf's story is, essentially, one of hope. Even in the most desperate circumstances, when threatened with losing his leg or being captured by the Taliban or being stranded at sea, Najaf hopes. A combination of good fortune and hope enables Najaf to achieve the 'impossible things' he enjoys at the narrative's conclusion.

The significance of hope to Najaf's story is evident in the two metaphors that bookend the narrative. When we first meet Najaf in Woomera, he discovers hope has returned to his heart. Likening hope to the perennial and hardy flowers in Mazar-e-Sharif, Najaf marvels at its resilience. After being reunited with Hakima and Maria, Najaf steals a few moments of quiet reflection outside the airport. Here, he contemplates the durability of his dreams, and comments that 'dreams that were dreamt in Afghanistan have put down roots in the soil of another nation, and today I see buds forming on twigs and branches' (p.248). Both images hint at the sensation of hope and evoke its productivity. Things grow out of hope.

Humility

Key quote

> 'It was not a huge dream, but a modest one, for it seemed to me that in the plans of God, I had been given a modest part to play.' (p.166)

Najaf is a humble and modest man. His humility is important because it significantly informs his narration of his story. There is no suggestion in the text that Najaf's experience of conflict is unique or any more remarkable than that of millions of people who have lived through similar things in Afghanistan or in other parts of the world.

This is achieved, in part, by the narrator's recurrent use of the inclusive pronoun 'we' instead of the individual 'I'. For example, the narrator speaks of 'all of us refugees' in Woomera (p.25) and of the return of the Taliban to Mazar-e-Sharif as an event 'we knew' would happen (p.182). It is also achieved by Najaf's deference to the experiences and thoughts of other people. The narrator, in describing the community in Woomera, directly states that the other asylum seekers from Iran or Chechnya or Kurdistan have the same experiences of explosions, death and grief as Najaf has had (p.26). Najaf's views on conflict are also presented as shared ideas. When he gives his appraisal of the mujahedin and the communists, for example, the narrator concludes that he had no powerful feelings about either side and that all he wants is to be left alone. He then states, 'I would say that my feelings … were not any different from those of most Afghanis' (p.150).

Nowhere is Najaf constructed as a particularly special, talented or unique individual. His peaceful and reasonable nature is modelled on and echoed by his older brother Gorg Ali. His family chooses to smuggle him out of Afghanistan because of pragmatic concerns, not favouritism. His successful flight to Australia is no more courageous than the similar ones made by the men, women and children with whom he shares the journey or with whom he lives at Woomera.

Najaf's survival is attributed more to luck than to special talents or traits. He attributes his survival to 'good fortune' (p.253). That many people just like him did not enjoy such luck weighs heavily on Najaf's conscience. What Najaf dubs 'the problem of my good fortune' (p.253) could be described as 'survivor's guilt', a psychological condition that occurs when a person perceives themself to have done wrong by surviving a traumatic event. Najaf is indeed engulfed by sadness when he thinks of Afghani people 'who deserved good fortune for the hard work they had accepted all their lives', but who had nevertheless died (p.253). However, his humility about his own survival is consistent with what is expressed elsewhere in the narrative.

DIFFERENT INTERPRETATIONS

Different interpretations arise from different responses to a text. Over time, a text will give rise to a wide range of responses from its readers, who may come from various social or cultural groups and live in very different places and historical periods. These responses can be published in newspapers, journals and books by critics and reviewers, or they can be expressed in discussions among readers in the media, classrooms, book groups and so on. While there is no single correct reading or interpretation of a text, it is important to understand that an interpretation is more than a personal opinion: it is the justification of a point of view on the text. To present an interpretation of the text based on your point of view you must use a logical argument and support it with relevant evidence from the text.

Critical viewpoints

The Rugmaker of Mazar-e-Sharif is a collaborative autobiography that details the life of a man with an astonishing story. However, Najaf is not famous, and Hillman, though respected, is not among Australia's pre-eminent authors. Therefore, when *The Rugmaker of Mazar-e-Sharif* was published in 2008, it received only a modicum of media interest. Further, it is a relatively new text and does not have the weight of decades of scholarship behind it, as a text by Shakespeare, Charles Dickens or even Tim Winton might. In short, there is not a great deal of published critical work about the text.

What little there is comes from a handful of columnists who reviewed *The Rugmaker of Mazar-e-Sharif* in some of Australia's major newspapers. Tim Johnston wrote about the text for *The Australian*; Bruce Elder reviewed it in *The Sydney Morning Herald*; Thuy On appraised it in *The Age;* and Verna McGeachin expressed her opinion in the *Sun-Herald.*

These reviewers all agree that the key achievement of the text is that it gives a name, a face and an identity to refugees. As McGeachin writes, Najaf's autobiography 'explains more about illegal immigrants than any newspaper headline'. This common appraisal is a response to what On dubs a 'political expedient' of the Howard government, which in 2001 instituted controversial policies that became widely known as 'the Pacific solution'. On contends that this policy relied upon grouping refugees 'into an amorphous mass'. Elder states that Najaf's story 'deserves to be read by everyone who was ashamed at the way Australia treated refugees' during that time. Johnston, however, shies away from overtly political statements, and suggests the text itself demonstrates a conspicuous tentativeness to engage in political argument.

Johnston contends that the text's apparent simplicity steers it away from becoming openly political. He suggests the narrator's 'naive and determined' voice 'allows the authors to tread paths that would be dangerously slippery to more knowing writers'. Elder has a different view. He proposes that Hillman is, in fact, highly aware of the political implications of Najaf's story. He states Hillman is 'quietly furious about the Howard government's treatment of refugees' and is 'determined to put a human face to the hardships endured by refugees'. Elder suggests Hillman 'has found an Afghani rug-maker' whose story is used to vent his fury.

Johnston and Elder clearly have divergent understandings of the authorship of *The Rugmaker of Mazar-e-Sharif*. Elder conceptualises the text as biography, with Hillman as its sole author. On has a similar view, stating that the text is 'strictly a biography' in which Najaf provides the 'raw materials' and Hillman the skills to 'weave … a coherent story'. Johnston, however, views Najaf's and Hillman's roles as more collaborative. He dubs Hillman an amanuensis (a person who writes only from dictation) and his review discusses 'Mazari's' voice and ideas, in contrast to Elder's review which consistently refers to Hillman as the writer and Najaf as the subject.

Perhaps this distinction explains why Johnston's review expresses more interest in Najaf than those by Elder, On and McGeachin. Johnston gives an outline of Najaf's character, describing his 'exceptional humility', his unwavering faith and his compassion. Writing for *M/C Reviews*, Elizabeth Emmanuel takes a similar line. She refers to Najaf's optimism, patience and 'unpretentious wisdom' and describes him as a man who 'seems almost incapable of rage'.

Johnston is also perhaps the most admiring reviewer. In a second article published in *The Australian*, Johnston reviews *The Rugmaker of Mazar-e-Sharif* alongside other publications that take Afghanistan as their setting and its culture and perpetual conflict as their themes (Sally Cooper's *A Burqua and a Hard Place* and Asne Seierstad's *The Bookseller of Kabul*). Johnston declares Najaf's autobiography a 'landmark' publication because it 'delivers the Afghanis from the tyranny of Western preconceptions'. On also touches on this, remarking that the text 'offers insight into the daily customs and rituals of agricultural Afghan life'.

Two interpretations

Interpretation 1: *The Rugmaker of Mazar-e-Sharif* depicts the life of an extraordinary individual.

Autobiography typically celebrates the lives of extraordinary people. *The Rugmaker of Mazar-e-Sharif* is no exception. Its protagonist, Najaf Mazari, is a truly remarkable man. Although the text attempts to construct this character as ordinary and representative of his Afghani and refugee communities, Najaf's beliefs, traits and achievements mark him as an extraordinary individual.

Najaf is born into a climate of ceaseless conflict. Successive wars, perpetuated by a cycle of violence and vengeance, rage in his homeland of Afghanistan. To many of Najaf's compatriots, 'individual honour and the honour of their tribe is so deeply rooted in their hearts that there is nothing on earth that they would not do to preserve it' (p.36). These are young Najaf's role models – angry, vengeful men who are 'the best in the world at close-range fighting' (p.175).

Given this background, it is a mark of Najaf's capacity for tolerance and acceptance that he can describe himself as a man of peace. Peace 'is part of me,' he claims, 'something that was inside of my brain and my heart when my mother gave birth to me' (p.76). Najaf's assessment of himself as a peaceful man is borne out in his relationships with others. For example, in Woomera detention centre he deliberately creates situations that guarantee peace among the tense refugee group. He smiles at everyone, ensures every inmate receives an equal serve of food and later puts an Afghani in charge of serving so no claims of partisanship can be made.

That Najaf is an exceptional inmate in Woomera is obvious in his election to a leadership position. He is made a mess supervisor and a leader of his Afghani group (p.71). His outstanding qualities also recommend him to shipmates aboard the derelict boat that conveys refugees to Australia. He is quickly elected as a group leader, in charge of ensuring his group adheres to the boat's rules, rules that 'were all to do with behaving peacefully and honestly' (p.234). Indeed, Najaf would not be on that boat if not for his superior traits. Najaf's family pool their meagre resources to pay a people smuggler to spirit him out of Afghanistan. The family can only raise enough money to pay for one escape. Najaf, because of his level-headedness and quick thinking (described in the text humbly as 'luck'), is 'the chosen one' (p.220). His extraordinary traits are the foundation for the esteem in which Najaf is demonstrably held.

Najaf's achievements also mark him as extraordinary. Once settled in Melbourne, he quickly establishes a rug business and successfully negotiates Australian business law and practice, despite his limited English. Najaf's determination, drive and discipline are obvious at an early age. He commits to his rugmaking apprenticeship at twelve and exhibits a sobriety of character that is, as evidenced by the contrast with Rosal Ali's behaviour, exceptional. That Najaf continues his apprenticeship, eventually becoming a master rugmaker despite the caprices of conflict, illustrates his exemplary determination.

Najaf's story itself is nothing new. It is a story we have heard many times before – fearing for his life, a refugee seeks asylum in Australia, endures the strictures of Australia's detainment system, attains citizenship and, once settled and reunited with his family, ultimately makes good. What is exceptional about Najaf's story is Najaf himself. If *The Rugmaker of Mazar-e-Sharif* raises any question about Australia's refugee policy, it is this: are we willing to put up with a system that would exclude individuals with the drive and determination exhibited by the extraordinary Najaf Mazari?

Interpretation 2: *The Rugmaker of Mazar-e-Sharif* enhances our understanding of refugees' experiences by telling a representative story of one ordinary man.

Autobiography is usually the domain of exceptional people. *The Rugmaker of Mazar-e-Sharif* is an unusual example of the genre because its protagonist is exceptionally ordinary. The memoir tells a remarkable story of danger, despair and determination, but its central character is carefully and deliberately depicted as unexceptional.

The text's protagonist, Najaf Mazari, lives through seemingly extraordinary events in war-torn Afghanistan. However extraordinary these situations might seem to a reader blessed with safety and security, Najaf, in narrating his experiences, carefully conveys their ordinariness for people like himself. After decades of incessant fighting, Afghanis, Najaf explains, perceive warfare as 'a disaster so common that it was useless to think of it as something that could be avoided' (p.129). Najaf does not even suggest that this familiarity with conflict is peculiar to Afghanistan. In Woomera, he observes 'it was a mujahedin explosion that killed my younger brother but others here have had family members killed by Russian explosions in Chechnya, or Iraqi explosions in Kurdistan' (p.26). While the settings are different, the consequent suffering is the same. Najaf's experiences are no different from those of other people who encounter conflict.

The explanation of Najaf's survival further demonstrates his ordinariness. Najaf does not escape the Taliban because of any special talents or character traits. His survival is attributed to one thing: good fortune. Najaf's evident luck is the clinching factor in the Mazari family's decision to smuggle him, rather than another family member, out of Afghanistan. Najaf recounts, 'I was considered lucky. I had survived the rocket attack, I had managed to keep out of the hands of the militias … and I had come back from the dead after falling into the hands of the Taliban' (p.220). Najaf is not constructed as a hero simply because he survives conflict.

It could be argued that Najaf is exceptional because he remains a man of peace despite war's toll. The text shows that fighting is a way of life for many Afghani men. Najaf describes, for instance, the attitude of certain men who would 'commit themselves and a hundred generations of their family to battle' just to preserve their honour (p.36). With such a background, it is remarkable that Najaf remains, by description and action, a peaceable man. But even here, he is not an exception. The character of Qadem, a Pashtun and traditional enemy of Najaf's Hazara people, demonstrates that others survive conflict with their humanity unscathed. Qadem, who knows Najaf, arranges his escape out of Afghanistan.

Neither are Najaf's beliefs unique. His assessment of war is modelled on the pronouncements of his eldest brother. It is Gorg Ali who first describes anger as 'a hammer' and who perceives that one person's passion and anger 'simply aroused the same sort of passion and anger in another' (pp.10–11). Similarly, Najaf's irrepressible hope and resilience are in fact community attributes. It is not only Najaf, but 'the people of Afghanistan' who live 'as if a normal life [is] still possible', making plans for the future, getting married, having children and building houses (p.164). The depiction of life in Woomera also shows that resilience is a common human trait, not one unique to Najaf. Though Najaf's beliefs and attitudes are commendable, they are nowhere presented as qualities unique to the protagonist.

Najaf is not an extraordinary man. At least, he is no more extraordinary than other survivors of conflict whom he symbolically represents in *The Rugmaker of Mazar-e-Sharif*. Najaf is a representative character, a conduit who gives a human face and story to the millions of civilians who live through conflict and to those refugees who, for political expediency, are so often regarded as a nameless, faceless mass.

QUESTIONS & ANSWERS

This section focuses on your own analytical writing on the text, and gives you strategies for producing high quality responses in your coursework and exam essays.

Essay writing – an overview

An essay is a formal and serious piece of writing that presents your point of view on the text, usually in response to a given essay topic. Your 'point of view' in an essay is your interpretation of the meaning of the text's language, structure, characters, situations and events, supported by detailed analysis of textual evidence.

Analyse – don't summarise

In your essays it is important to avoid simply summarising what happens in a text:

- A **summary** is a description or paraphrase (retelling in different words) of the characters and events. For example: 'Macbeth has a horrifying vision of a dagger dripping with blood before he goes to murder King Duncan'.
- An **analysis** is an explanation of the real meaning or significance that lies 'beneath' the text's words (and images, for a film). For example: 'Macbeth's vision of a bloody dagger shows how deeply uneasy he is about the violent act he is contemplating – as well as his sense that supernatural forces are impelling him to act'.

A limited amount of summary is sometimes necessary to let your reader know which part of the text you wish to discuss. However, always keep this to a minimum and follow it immediately with your analysis (explanation) of what this part of the text is really telling us.

Plan your essay

Carefully plan your essay so that you have a clear idea of what you are going to say. The plan ensures that your ideas flow logically, that your argument remains consistent and that you stay on the topic. An essay plan should be a list of brief dot points – no more than half a page. It includes:

- **your central argument or main contention** – a concise statement (usually in a single sentence) of your overall response to the topic. See 'Analysing a sample topic' for guidelines on how to formulate a main contention.
- **three or four dot points for each paragraph** indicating the main idea and evidence/examples from the text. Note that in your essay you will need to *expand* on these points and *analyse* the evidence.

Structure your essay

An essay is a complete, self-contained piece of writing. It has a clear beginning (the introduction), middle (several body paragraphs) and end (the last paragraph or conclusion). It must also have a central argument that runs throughout, linking each paragraph to form a coherent whole.

See examples of introductions and conclusions in the 'Analysing a sample topic' and 'Sample answer' sections.

The introduction establishes your overall response to the topic. It includes your main contention and outlines the main evidence you will refer to in the course of the essay. Write your introduction after you have done a plan and before you write the rest of the essay.

The body paragraphs argue your case – they present evidence from the text and explain how this evidence supports your argument. Each body paragraph needs:

- a strong **topic sentence** (usually the first sentence) that states the main point being made in the paragraph
- **evidence** from the text, including some brief quotations

- **analysis** of the textual evidence explaining its significance and **explanation** of how it supports your argument
- **links back to the topic** in one or more statements, usually towards the end of the paragraph.

Connect the body paragraphs so that your discussion flows smoothly. Use some linking words and phrases like 'similarly' and 'on the other hand', though don't start every paragraph in this way. Another strategy is to use a significant word from the last sentence of one paragraph in the first sentence of the next.

Use key terms from the topic – or synonyms for them – throughout, so the relevance of your discussion to the topic is always clear.

The conclusion ties everything together and finishes the essay. It includes strong statements that emphasise your central argument and provide a clear response to the topic.

Avoid simply restating the points made earlier in the essay – this will end on a very flat note and imply that you have run out of ideas and vocabulary. The conclusion is meant to be a logical extension of what you have written, not just a repetition or summary of it. Writing an effective conclusion can be a challenge. Try using these tips:

- Start by linking back to the final sentence of the second-last paragraph – this helps your writing to 'flow', rather than just leaping back to your main contention straight away.
- Use synonyms and expressions with equivalent meanings to vary your vocabulary. This allows you to reinforce your line of argument without being repetitive.
- When planning your essay, think of one or two broad statements or observations about the text's wider meaning. These should be related to the topic and your overall argument. Keep them for the conclusion, since they will give you something 'new' to say but still follow logically from your discussion. The introduction will be focused on the topic, but the conclusion can present a wider view of the text.

Essay topics

1 "War had always been the background to my life ... and it surely helped to form the way I thought about things." How is Najaf shaped by conflict?

2 '*The Rugmaker of Mazar-e-Sharif* argues that the causes of conflict matter less than its consequences.' Discuss.

3 'Najaf is an ordinary man in extraordinary circumstances.' To what extent does the text support this view?

4 'A person's present is always informed by their past.' How does *The Rugmaker of Mazar-e-Sharif* present the relationship between Najaf's past and present?

5 'We learn a lot about people through their relationships with others.' What do Najaf's relationships with other characters tell us about him?

6 '*The Rugmaker of Mazar-e-Sharif* is the story of one man overcoming enormous challenges.' How does the narrative structure of *The Rugmaker of Mazar-e-Sharif* convey Najaf's achievements?

7 '*The Rugmaker of Mazar-e-Sharif* dispels rather than accentuates cultural differences.' Discuss.

8 'It is impossible to fully comprehend conflict as a bystander.' Discuss.

9 'One conflict always contains the seeds of another.' To what extent does the text support this idea?

10 'The text shows that hope can overcome powerlessness.' Discuss.

Vocabulary for writing on *The Rugmaker of Mazar-e-Sharif*

Allegory: a story with both a primary and secondary meaning that can be read, understood and interpreted at two or more levels. The story of Kandhi Hazara is an example of allegory.

Autobiography: an account of a person's life told retrospectively by that person.

Biography: an account of a person's life written by another person.

Collaborative autobiography: an autobiography produced by the work of two or more people, but which uses a single narrator.

Fable: a short, allegorical tale intended to convey a moral.

Perspective: point of view or way of regarding some thing or situation.

Analysing a sample topic

'*The Rugmaker of Mazar-e-Sharif* dispels rather than accentuates cultural differences.' Discuss.

- First, identify and underline the key words in the statement. This helps you clarify what the question is really about. Here, you would probably underline: dispels, accentuates, cultural differences.
- Spend a few moments thinking about what these words mean. You might like to brainstorm some definitions, synonyms and examples from the text that immediately come to mind. Look up any words with which you are not familiar.
- Look for different elements to the question. Is there more than one aspect that needs to be considered? There are two elements here – that the text both accentuates and dispels difference. A strong answer will consider both aspects and examine the tension between them.

- Think about what the statement assumes. Are cultural differences evident in the text? Are these dispelled?
- Form your own opinion about the statement. Do you agree? Do you disagree? Remember, you are not required simply to agree with the statement. You need to form your own contention and develop a convincing argument using evidence from your reading of the text.
- Modify the statement so that it reflects your contention. Your modified statement should encapsulate the argument you intend to make. A response to this question might contend that 'Differences are accentuated to help the reader understand Najaf and his experiences, but the reader's ability to identify with him shows that cultural differences can be overcome. Therefore the text both accentuates and dispels differences.'

Sample introduction

> *The Rugmaker of Mazar-e-Sharif* recounts Najaf's journey from living with conflict in Afghanistan to living a safe and secure life in Australia, two markedly different cultures. To understand Najaf, and to comprehend the magnitude of his experiences as a refugee, the reader must be aware of the significant differences between Afghani and Australian cultures. The text, therefore, accentuates differences. However, because these are accentuated to help the reader better understand and sympathise with the protagonist, Najaf's story actually diminishes cultural differences. The reader is able to identify with Najaf and is able to understand his point of view, even though it might be very different from the reader's own.

Body paragraph outline

Body paragraph 1: Accentuation of cultural differences helps us understand Najaf's situation.

- Confusion in Woomera: Najaf has no birth certificate, only a taskera; no understanding of 'queue jumping'; strangeness of teabags, Australian bread and stickers on apples.
- Interview: highlights how easily misunderstandings can arise, and how significant cultural differences can become in particular situations. Evidences the precariousness of Najaf's situation.
- Summary: elucidation of differences here helps us understand how foreign and frightening Australia seems to Najaf – engages reader sympathy.

Body paragraph 2: Deliberate diminishment of difference also helps us comprehend what Najaf endures.

- Passage about the 'Woomerians' rebuilding Australia: they have the same hopes, dreams, needs.
- Outline that Najaf gives of Woomera community: particularly that it is composed of professional people, children, women etc. who continue to fall in love, have children etc. Same aspirations and same major events in life.
- Use of 'us' and 'we' in Najaf's comments about the community at Woomera. He links their experience to his: diminishes difference between himself and Iranians, Chechnyans etc. Helps the reader sympathise with the whole community as an extension of Najaf.
- Summary: refugees are 'humanised' and commonalities are established. The reader can identify with what might otherwise be a nameless and faceless crowd. This enables the reader to put themselves in Najaf's place and thereby appreciate the enormity of his experiences.

Body paragraph 3: Accentuation of cultural differences assists in characterisation of Najaf.

- Inclusion of fables: for example, King's Son and the Canary Birds, story about the camel. These succinctly communicate Najaf's way of looking at things and explain some of his key values and character traits.
- Portrayal of child employment: as a shepherd, apprentice blacksmith and apprentice rugmaker. This provides a foundation for Najaf's industrious and sober nature.
- Depiction of tradition: for example, the wedding Najaf attends as a boy, building of the house in Mazar-e-Sharif, Najaf's own wedding. Evokes a longing for a centuries-old way of life and exemplifies what Najaf has lost in leaving Afghanistan. Consider the statement: 'Can I ever feel the truth about myself in Australia?'
- Summary: outlining difference helps us appreciate Najaf's point of view, rather than view him as foreign or alien.

Body paragraph 4: Accentuation of cultural differences highlights what Najaf achieves in Australia.

- Once settled in Melbourne, Najaf experiences new things: observations from a bus window about the way people walk, drivers obeying traffic lights, learning about tax laws and EFTPOS, telephone calls with potential flatmates.
- Achievements: for example, rug shop and rented home show that Najaf is able to negotiate complex systems and practices in Australia.
- Friendships with Robin and Colin show cultural differences are not a barrier and that respect, goodwill and humour can override cultural divisions. Colin is particularly interesting here – consider characterisation and language: he is particularly 'Aussie'. That Najaf, a man so steeped in Afghani tradition, forms an equal friendship with Colin shows that cultural differences can be overcome.

- Change of tone: here more humorous, delighted, whereas in Woomera the differences were conveyed with confusion and despondency. Also, fewer differences are articulated here. Differences actually diminish as Australia becomes less strange to Najaf and as he makes friendships with Australian people.
- Summary: the reader sees some fairly typical practices (such as calling up about a flat or using EFTPOS) through fresh eyes; illuminates how culturally specific these things are and forces recognition of how much Najaf has overcome.

Sample conclusion

Cultural difference is certainly accentuated in *The Rugmaker of Mazar-e-Sharif*. Disparities between Afghani and Australian cultures are elucidated in the narrator's description of traditional Afghani life and customs, in the inclusion of traditional fables and in the protagonist's confusion as he attempts to adjust to life in Woomera and later in Melbourne. However, this accentuation of difference ultimately works to diminish difference. Appreciating cultural differences ensures the reader understands and empathises with Najaf. It is through accentuating these differences that Najaf's situation, character and achievements are made comprehensible to the average Australian reader.

SAMPLE ANSWER

'It is impossible to fully comprehend conflict as a bystander.' Discuss.

The Rugmaker of Mazar-e-Sharif is a civilian's memoir of encountering conflict. Najaf is a bystander to Afghanistan's wars. Not only does Najaf fully comprehend the horrors of conflict, but his position as a bystander actually enables him to develop and convey a more comprehensive picture of war than a combatant could. This is evident in Najaf's thorough evocation of conflict's immediate consequences, his depiction of how war shapes civilian communities and his attitudes about the purpose and justness of war.

Najaf is inarguably characterised as a bystander. He refuses to join the army when conscripting soldiers attempt to recruit him. His repudiation of active duty is not only due to his youth, but also to his categorical objection to fighting. Fighting does not build anything, Najaf contends, but 'will only tear down what others have built', an attitude modelled on the views of his much-admired brother Gorg Ali. His position as a bystander is further developed by description of him as a 'witness' to explosions. Najaf is an unwilling spectator to Afghanistan's wars.

Despite this position, Najaf gains a thorough comprehension of armed conflict's immediate effects. He is injured in a mortar attack on his family home. His younger brother is killed in this attack. Gorg Ali is killed a year earlier, struck by a sniper's bullet during a skirmish between the mujahedin and Soviet forces. Ultimately, Najaf is forced to flee his homeland. The text also captures the long-term consequences of these immediate costs. Najaf not only endures pain when his leg is injured, but also experiences a setback in his apprenticeship, financial hardship and resultant shame and despondency. Similarly, his flight from Afghanistan leads him on a dangerous journey; lands him in Woomera Detention Centre where he endures the anxiety of interminable waiting; and enables him to live in Australia, a country he comes to call home, but in which he doubts he can 'ever feel the truth' about himself. Although Najaf is a civilian and a bystander to conflict, he encounters and thus understands its many immediate consequences and their long-term effects.

Najaf's participation in civilian society endows him with a privileged perspective on conflict's effects on communities. Soldiers absorbed in fighting could not notice the powerlessness Najaf experiences, articulated in his resigned realisation that his future as a rugmaker depends entirely on circumstances outside of his control. Nor would soldiers know that decades of war have led to men building houses with specially designed cupboards for hiding from enemies, like the one in Ashraf's house, or know that young men like Najaf and Gassen adapt their senses in response to perpetual threat, eating with their 'ears pricked for the sound of [their] enemies' and easily woken 'by a stone rolling down a slope half a kilometre away'. Najaf's civilian experience of war allows him to comprehend and demonstrate its social and psychological costs.

But perhaps the aspect of conflict that Najaf is able to comprehend far more fully than a combatant is its futility and unjustness. Focused on military goals and targets, a soldier might not conceptualise war as pointless. To Najaf, however, who witnesses so many successive conflicts that he compares the warring parties to boxers who would fight until one 'would finally fall down dead, but the other would be a cripple for the rest of his life', war is unquestionably futile. Five separate conflicts occur during Najaf's lifetime, but peace is never attained, only an occasional balance. From experience he predicts Afghanistan 'will be at war for a long time to come'.

Cognisant of war's futility, Najaf comprehends another aspect of conflict of which combatants would likely be ignorant: its unjustness. Najaf implies that, at least during Afghanistan's civil war, 'both sides expected that it would be necessary to kill civilians, or at least that it would be too troublesome to avoid killing them'. Najaf exposes the terrible unfairness of this, summed up in his description of Afghanistan as an 'explosion laboratory', his statement that Afghanistan is 'supposed to fit into the political strategies of the powerful', and the lament that

Afghanis have not 'chosen a path of suffering out of madness' but that 'other people have chosen that path for us'. The senselessness and unfairness of war are aspects of conflict that Najaf can only comprehend because he is a bystander.

Najaf is unquestionably a bystander to conflict, both by persuasion and characterisation. This standpoint allows him to gain a full understanding of conflict. He not only experiences conflict's immediate and long-term consequences, but also perceives how it touches communities. Ultimately, his civilian encounter with conflict enables him to comprehend aspects of conflict to which combatants would be inured: its futility and unjustness.

The Rugmaker of Mazar-e-Sharif shows that, far from it being impossible to fully comprehend conflict as a bystander, certain elements of conflict can only be discerned by someone who merely witnesses and endures its effects. In this way, a bystander can be said to have a privileged perspective on conflict.

REFERENCES & READING

Text

Mazari, N and R Hillman 2008, *The Rugmaker of Mazar-e-Sharif*, Wild Dingo Press, Melbourne.

Journal articles

Hillman, R 2007, 'Beyond pity', *Griffith Review*, vol. 15, autumn, pp.209–20.

Varga, S 2009, 'Dark times', *Griffith Review*, vol. 24, winter, pp.173–80.

Newspaper articles

Elder, B 2008, 'The rugmaker of Mazar-e-Sharif', *Sydney Morning Herald*, 2 May, www.smh.com.au/news/book-reviews/the-rugmaker-of-mazaresharif/2008/05/02/1209235136473.html

Johnston, T 2008, 'One man's journey a tale of our times', *The Australian*, 10 May, https://web.archive.org/web/20090310160937/http://www.theaustralian.news.com.au/story/0,25197,23654377-5003900,00.html

Johnston, T 2008, 'Deliver them from preconceptions', *The Australian*, 2 July, pp.8–10.

McGeachin, V 2008, 'Memoir', *Sun-Herald*, 18 May, p.11.

On, T 2008, 'Weft and weave of an asylum seeker', *The Age*, 3 May, p.23.

Websites

Emanuel, E 2008, 'Memoir: *The Rugmaker of Mazar-e-Sharif* by Najaf Mazari', *M/C Reviews*, https://web.archive.org/web/20110413101419/https://reviews.media-culture.org.au/modules.php?name=News&file=article&sid=2608

Mazari, N and R Hillman 2009, *The Rugmaker of Mazar-e-Sharif*, ABC Perth, www.abc.net.au/local/audio/2009/02/28/2501438.htm (a podcast of a presentation given by Najaf and Robert at the 2009 Perth Writers Festival)